Learn to Do
Appliqué
in Just One Weekend

By Nancy Brenan Daniel

HOUSE of
WHITE
BIRCHES
PUBLISHERS
SINCE 1947

About the Author

Certified as a teacher and a judge by The National Quilting Association Inc., Nancy Brenan Daniel has been teaching quiltmaking since 1975 at workshops and during major national and international quilting events. She has written and designed several books about hand quilting, appliqué and rotary techniques. Nancy has appeared on television shows demonstrating her various special techniques. She frequently appears as a designer and author in exhibitions, books and magazines. She co-owned a quilt shop for almost 10 years and currently holds memberships in several professional quilting and writing organizations.

Nancy began her professional life as an art teacher. It was a natural step for her to eventually direct her creative and teaching talents to the art of quiltmaking. She is a graduate of the University of Alabama and received her master's degree from Arizona State University in art history.

Nancy is a traditional and studio quiltmaker, designer and teacher. Her interest in quilts began in childhood. She is the granddaughter of lifelong quilter, Mary Talkington Ritzenthaler of Columbus, Ind. Her mother, Mary Brenan, finished her first quilt at age 75 and her second quilt at 82. Upon her death, she left Nancy an unfinished quilt top in a Bow Tie design. Nancy has layered this quilt and hand-quilts a little on it from time to time. She is mother to three adult children—Karen, David and Stephen. Her current dog, Sasha is a rescued Border Collie. Together, they live in the Arizona desert.

Acknowledgements

I wish to offer my sincerest and heartfelt thanks to the following, without whom this book would not have been possible:

All those who have participated in the folkloric appliqué workshops for many years—especially the First Friday and First Tuesday groups at The Quilters' Ranch in Tempe, Ariz. Your questions and enthusiasm have kept me on my toes.

To the thousands of anonymous folk artists throughout history who interpret nature and human ideas into delightful images.

To the contemporary artists and quilters who have shared their special stories and reference materials.

To the early authors and teachers who taught us to hold onto and expand the quiltmaking tradition and to the authors and teachers of today who continue to explore and create new tools and techniques.

To the publishers and the editors who contributed their talents during the preparation of this material and book. Thank you for being patient, allowing me to find my voice, and helping me to focus.

To family members and friends who encourage and love me.

To all of you—many thanks.

HOUSE of WHITE BIRCHES
PUBLISHERS SINCE 1947

ISBN: 978-1-59217-329-7

1 2 3 4 5 6 7 8 9

Introduction

Appliqué quilts made today rival the best in our tradition, and they are made using easier techniques with modern tools and supplies.

The tools and supplies available today make life easier for appliqué quiltmakers, and as a result they help to make superior quilts. The contemporary art of the appliqué quilt has been the beneficiary of many good books, designers, good instruction in the techniques and the use of old and new tools.

An appliqué quilt has patches made up of one or several fabrics that are applied to a background fabric with a stitching or fusing method. Appliqué designs often exhibit the expressive curves of nature, tools, toys and other shapes. They are frequently things not particularly suited to the geometric design of ordinary patchwork.

This book contains a variety of techniques for appliqué that I've used and taught over many years. Some of them are fast and some are not, but they all serve a purpose in quiltmaking. Because many of my students once referred to appliqué as the "A" word, I am determined to convert them with cleanly designed, playful patterns and easy instructions.

My own early introduction to appliqué was not a positive one. Grandmother Ritzenthaler did not appliqué, and she didn't have many kind words for quilters having the time to make what she considered "fancy quilts." After all, she had raised six children through a world war and a depression.

There are not many family-appliqué quilts, but I certainly saw them being aired on neighbors' wash lines around my grandmother's home in Indiana, and I liked what I saw. Appliqué quilts are interesting and attractive—even Grandma would admit that.

Grandma compromised her beliefs about appliqué when I went away to university. She made me a Dresden Plate quilt in red and white—the colors of my school. She did it again when our daughter was born by making her a crib quilt embellished with kittens and embroidery.

I had made our daughter-to-be a sensible patchwork quilt, but within six months of the birth of our first child, I began my lifelong quest for the easiest methods of appliqué.

I wish I could say that my early research was purely experimental and artistic. It was, however, a very practical and down-to-earth need to quickly mend and cushion the knees in Karen's crawlers—I might add that this was before the arrival of fusible webbing. To create the padding that was needed, and to make it easier to apply the heart or bunny-shaped patches, I started to face the patches with nylon bridal tulle; it was lightweight and inexpensive, and I could stuff padding in it before I applied the patch. The facing technique was then, and still is, a great technique.

This book is written for use as a technical guide to traditional and contemporary techniques used by appliqué quiltmakers today. Quilters wanting tips and answers about improving their own appliqué techniques, as well as learning new techniques, will find many helpful suggestions.

The folkloric appliqué designs in this collection are images of universal appeal for decorative arts. They are simple images that share the symbolism of fine appliqué and other art, but I've created or re-designed them following the sage advice, forgiving nature, and good humor of my students. I hope your adventure with appliqué will be fun-filled and produce lively quilts.

House of White Birches, Berne, Indiana 46711 Clotilde.com

How to Make an Appliqué Quilt

Planning & Inspiration for Original Quilts

Selecting your patterns and planning your appliqué quilt project can be exciting or daunting depending on your outlook and experience.

The designs and projects I've chosen, pre-planned, and made for this book incorporate much of my philosophy regarding appliqué design, teaching of beginning and intermediate appliqué techniques and quiltmaking. You'll discover that I prefer appliqué equally integrated with patchwork, that I often design more than one border for a quilt, and that I like clearly defined images.

As a teacher, I prefer the learn-by-doing, practical approach. I also love it when students and quilters take liberties with my designs and make them their own.

Planning

If you are designing an original, plan every aspect of your quilt before you ever take a stitch. Make a sketch of the design—include the appliqué blocks, the patchwork, all borders and the quilting patterns. Make a simple line drawing or use colored pencils to add all the details. Figure out your fabric yardage, colors and order of appliqué placement. Keep good records of your ideas and "notes-to-self." You cannot plan too much.

On the other hand, you might want to start right off with a bit of background fabric and some appliqué patches and simply sew them down!

However you choose to work in appliqué—with wild abandon or complete control—the goal is to make something interesting and personal. Learn to have fun with the techniques.

Inspiration

With all of this work behind you, set the plans and drawings aside for a few days. Allow yourself time to reflect before you begin to cut and stitch.

Ponder—become inspired to make the project your own.

Have you coordinated elements of the central design with your borders and quilting? Does the design appear to be a unified whole, or does it look as if it is made up of unrelated parts? Is there a sense of harmony and balance? Is there enough contrast in each part of the design—will anyone mistake a rose, for example, with the heart it overlaps? Is your design interesting? Does it have some sparkle? Is it worth your effort to complete?

That last question may seem like a strange one, but I've seen many technically perfect quilts that are boring. Anyone with enough time could have sewn them.

Allow time and permission for inspiration in the process. Remember that creative plans are meant to be changed.

As you work on your appliqué quilts, you will discover your own favorite techniques and styles. I hope you will read widely about appliqué quilts and techniques. The more exposure you get the more likely you are to develop your own opinions and approaches to making quilts.

Keep an open mind and be willing to learn everything you can from as many teachers and books as possible, but with this single caution—develop your own style and color sense. If you want to appliqué purple leaves, go right ahead and do it—I give you permission!

Color & Visual Texture

There is only one rule regarding the choice of color or visual texture: There should be enough contrast between the background and the applied fabrics to clearly communicate the design.

The amount of contrast between the background and the applied fabrics is a matter of personal taste. Remember, however, that you want others to enjoy the designs you've chosen, so make sure there is enough contrast.

Notes for Success
The following list includes specific information to apply to your appliqué projects:

• All patchwork seams are sewn with right sides together unless otherwise stated.

• All seams are sewn with a ¼" seam allowance. In miniature designs, a ⅛" seam allowance is suggested.

• Press all seams toward the darker fabric in the appliqué.

• Press seams open in patchwork whenever practical and unless otherwise stated.

• Patterns for appliqué shapes do not include the seam allowance.

• Stitches used to apply the appliqué pieces should be firm and close together—no more than ⅛" apart. Stitches should not float on top of the appliqué or background fabric.

Terms
Specific terms are referenced throughout this book. The following list of terms applies to specific techniques used.

Finger-press: Open a stitched seam. Firmly, without stretching, press flat with the balls of your fingertips.

Strip Piecing: Sewing long strips of fabric together or to previously sewn units.

Chain Piecing: Sewing a complete group of one type of unit in one continuous, long chain.

Squaring a Block: Measuring, and trimming all blocks so they will be the same size, if necessary. Do not trim off the ¼" seam allowance.

Basic Supplies for Appliqué Quilts
Choose your notions and tools carefully. To begin, buy good quality, sharp needles, matching threads, embroidery scissors, 100 percent cotton fabrics and a good needle threader. You will discover for yourself any additional supplies and tools you need. Read through the appliqué techniques I've suggested for specific supply needs.

Appliqué Pins
Appliqué pins are thin and very sharp. They have

small heads. Another type of pin I like to use has a flattened disk for the pin head. The pin heads should be heat resistant.

Appliqué Foot
An open-channel sewing machine foot for machine appliqué.

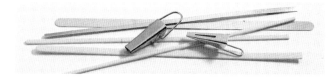

Bias Bars & Bias Tape Makers
Bias bars and bias tape makers aid in making various width bias tapes for making vines, stems and woven appliqué. The bars may be manufactured in metal or in heat-resistant nylon. These tools have set the standard for uniform and flowing stems and vines.

Facing Material
Nylon tulle and lightweight interfacing are used for quick turning of large, simple appliqué shapes. Do not use the fusible facings for appliqué. Use the same or a coordinating fabric for dimensional appliqué, page 12.

Fabric
For most projects, use 100 percent cotton. Cotton fabrics are stable and hold a fold when creased or pressed.

Fabrics should not fray when cut with scissors. Other kinds of fabrics may be used by experienced quilters for special projects.

Freezer Paper
Freezer paper is a coated paper that is used as a foundation for appliqué and for making cardboard templates. Find this product at any grocery store.

Fusible Webbing

Fusible webbing is a paper-backed fusible product that is used to permanently apply a fabric to the background fabric—with or without added stitching by hand or machine. This material comes in several weights. Read the manufacturer's suggestions for use and application directions before you buy.

There are several types of fusible webbing that come in various, very narrow widths, such as ¼" and ⅜". This type of narrow fusible web is perfect for applying stems.

Glue Sticks

Glue sticks can be found in tubes of permanent or repositionable and should be designed for fabric and acid free. Both types are useful to have.

Irons

In addition to a good steam iron, a small, travel-size iron or a specialized appliqué iron is helpful for finishing delicate appliqué edges.

Stitchless Sewing Liquid

Stitchless sewing liquid is a helpful product to help seal the raw edges of non-turned appliqué pieces and/or to baste appliqué pieces in place. An example of this product is Liquid Stitch.

Marking Tools

Rinse-out markers, silver pencils, soap slivers, and a variety of other non-permanent markers for dark and light fabrics are needed for appliqué. Do not use waxy dressmaker's pencils.

Use a very light touch when working with any marking tool. The marks made by these markers must be removed from the fabric when appliqué is completed.

Needles for Machine-Quilting & Appliqué

For machine quilting, appliqué and embroidery, use sharp needles in sizes 11–14.

For hand appliqué, use sharps. These are very fine, sharp, somewhat flexible, needles designed for hand stitching and appliqué. The points and eyes of these needles are long and very thin. Look at the eye of the needle and buy the one you can thread by "eye" or with the help of a needle threader. If you can't thread it, you can't use it.

Needles for Hand-Quilting

To quilt your project, use size 10, 11 or 12 between quilting needles. These needles are short and have a very small eye to help ease the needle through the extra layers when quilting. These needles are extra strong so they won't break easily when quilting.

Needle Grabber

A needle grabber is a rubber fingertip, available at office-supply stores, that helps you grip small needles and pins. Wear it on your index finger.

Needle Threader

A needle threader is a tool designed with a fine wire to pass through the eye of the needle and catch the thread. There are many variations on the market.

Try out before you buy if possible. Mechanical threaders are also available.

Open-Channel Machine-Appliqué Foot

An open-channel foot is a necessity for machine appliqué and most machine decorative stitches.

Overlay Materials

Use flexible plastic or vinyl for design overlays. Clear sheet protectors are inexpensive to use and readily available.

Permanent Markers

Permanent markers may be used when creating design overlays.

Rulers & Tape Measures

Rulers or tape measures are used for measuring when centering designs and for general measuring of the quilt and its parts.

Sandpaper

Use emery sandpaper or another very fine-grit sandpaper to prevent the appliqué fabric from shifting under the pencil when you mark it.

Scissors

General use cloth and paper scissors are needed. Small, sharp-pointed, embroidery scissors are used for detail work.

Stabilizers

Stabilizers are used to add support on the backside of machine appliqué. There are many types of commercial stabilizers for various kinds of fabrics. Tissue paper and freezer paper can also be used. Refer to your sewing machine instructions for the best choice for your project.

Starch

Liquid or spray starch is used to re-size fabrics and to treat some appliqué edges.

Template Materials

For appliqué and patchwork templates, use medium-weight plastic or poster board that is specifically created for this purpose, or manila file folders. Choose heat-resistant materials such as cardboard for appliqué templates as some techniques require the use of a heated iron with the template.

Thimble

A good-fitting thimble is suggested for hand appliqué, hand piecing and hand quilting. The thimble should be snug without pinching or applying pressure on the finger joint. Use on the middle finger of the dominant hand.

Threads

All-purpose, cotton, silk or monofilament thread can be used for appliqué. The thread should match the piece that is being applied. If an exact match can't be found, use a slightly duller or darker color to blend into the shadows of the appliqué.

Monofilament thread is a thread made from nylon or polyester that is strong and wears well. It comes in clear and smoky gray colors that blend with both the appliqué and the background fabrics, becoming virtually invisible.

Silk thread is very fine, strong and wears well except under high heat and long-term bright light.

There are specialized bobbin threads for appliqué and machine embroidery called bobbin fill. Bobbin fill is a fine thread available in black or white that reduces bulk and produces better stitches. It can be purchased in pre-wound bobbins.

Embroidery floss is a soft, decorative, 6-ply thread used for embellishment stitches such as the blanket stitch on edges of appliqué. Do not use embroidery floss to apply the fabric to the background. Use in decorative stitches only.

Wooden Toothpicks

Wooden toothpicks help in tucking pesky seam allowances under.

Nice-to-Have Tools or Supplies

Appliqué Scissors

Also called spoon scissors, these scissors are perfect for the fanatic appliqué artist! The special duck-bill blade protects underneath layers of fabric.

Hemostats or Long Tweezers

Hemostats or long tweezers are perfect for turning appliqué edges and removing freezer-paper templates from stitched units.

House of White Birches, Berne, Indiana 46711 Clotilde.com

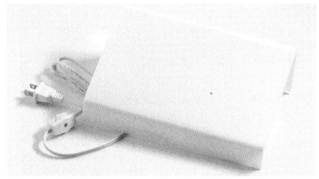

Light Table or Box

A light table or box is used to transfer the designs from paper to the background fabric. The light shining through the pattern makes it easier to transfer the design to the fabric.

If a light table or box isn't available, tape designs and fabric to a window for transferring the design, or use a heavy plastic sheet resting between two tables with a lamp placed below.

Making & Using Templates

Appliqué Templates

Create permanent appliqué templates for each pattern piece from thin template material. Draw or trace the outline of the pattern onto one of the suggested template materials. Add any markings and labels. Cut out the design using a craft knife or

sharp scissors. Appliqué templates do not include the seam allowance. Make a special note of overlapping and underlapping areas as shown in Figure 1.

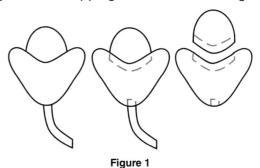

Figure 1

Window Templates

Window templates, shown in Figure 2, allow you to take the best advantage of your fabric.

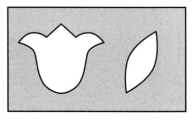

Figure 2

To make a window template, trace appliqué designs onto a piece of cardboard. Leave an inch or two between each shape. Cut the silhouettes out with a craft knife. Clearly label the right side of the template sheet.

To use the window template, place the template shape desired over the fabric and move it around until you've isolated the part of the fabric you want to feature in the template shape. Draw around shape using fabric pen or pencil.

Timely Tips

1. Make a photocopy of the appliqué design and glue the paper copy to the cardboard. Next, cut the patterns from the cardboard. This method creates the perfect size template labeled with all the pattern information.

2. Trace appliqué designs and information onto freezer paper. Iron the freezer paper, dull side down, onto the cardboard. Then cut the patterns from the cardboard.

3. For home-computer users, scan the appliqué designs and print out onto freezer paper cut to fit your printer. Iron printed freezer paper onto the cardboard and cut out the patterns.

Timely Tip

For added interest and visual texture, sew together different fabrics to create the desired effect. Use the window template to isolate the area you want, and then trace shape as shown in Figure 3.

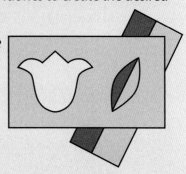

Figure 3

Caution: Many appliqué techniques will result in a reversing of the design when you transfer it to your fabric. Any asymmetrical design will reverse under some conditions. Practice playing with odd-shaped designs until you understand how this can happen. Some shapes can fool you! Learn to create a mirror image of your design, particularly for some fusible-web and freezer-paper techniques (Figure 4).

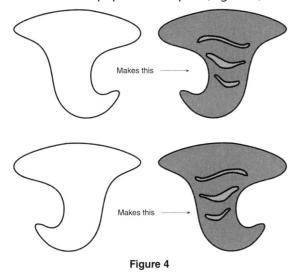

Figure 4

Patchwork Templates

Make patchwork templates from thin, stiff cardboard or template plastic. Draw or trace the outline of the pattern onto the template material. Cut out the design using a craft knife or sharp scissors. Add any markings or labels, referring to the Timely Tips for using appliqué designs.

Preparing Patches for Appliqué

Appliqué Techniques

There are many good techniques used for hand and machine appliqué. Talk to six needle workers who enjoy appliqué, and you will discover they might use a half-dozen or more similar techniques. What you might not discover is that even though they use the same techniques, they might choose to use them under differing circumstances. That's the art of appliqué—knowing when and how to use different techniques.

You will want to examine, explore and practice the various techniques that I suggest for beginning and intermediate appliqué quiltmakers. They are "almost-no-fail" techniques that are forgiving and allow one to easily correct most mistakes. I'm not a beginning appliqué quiltmaker, and these are still the techniques I prefer to teach and use most often.

As you make more appliqué quilts and projects, you will discover other techniques to try, and you will probably invent a few new ones for yourself—this art lends itself to inspiration, innovation and imagination!

Several techniques are described in the following section. Each of these techniques is suitable for any of the projects in this book.

Begin with pre-washed fabric that has been ironed and re-sized/starched for stability.

Three Freezer-Paper Techniques
Number 1: Dull Side Down—Wrong Side of Fabric

This technique uses freezer-paper templates to hold seam allowances of appliqué pieces in place.

1. Trace around the appliqué template onto the dull side of the freezer paper.

2. Cut the actual shape from the paper. Do not add a seam allowance.

3. Pin the freezer-paper piece dull side down against the wrong side of the fabric. Using a sharp hard pencil or stylus, trace around the template to crease the seam-allowance fold line. Cut the fabric around the shape, leaving a ¼" seam allowance.

4. Clip into the seam allowances almost to the creased line. Clip only on the inside curves and "V" areas as shown in Figure 5—clip as little as possible.

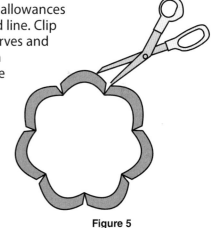

Figure 5

5. With the point of a hot iron, press the seam allowance over the edge of the paper. The heat will stick the fabric to the shiny side of the freezer paper. Move along the seam-allowance edge carefully to create smooth curves and crisp points. Move slowly, pressing only a little bit at a time (Figure 6). Remove any excess fabric at the "V"s.

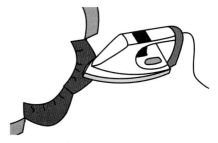

Figure 6

6. Place prepared pieces in a plastic bag to protect them until they are ready to use. If the shape is very complicated, or you do not plan to use it soon, remove the freezer-paper template, repress the seam allowance and thread- or glue-baste the edges down.

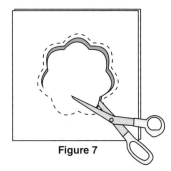

Figure 7

7. After the pieces have been stitched to the background, turn to the underside and cut away the background fabric under the appliqué pieces, leaving a ¼" seam allowance as shown in Figure 7. Remove freezer-paper template if you have not previously removed it.

Timely Tip

Draw Once—Cut Many! Referring to Figure 8, cut a strip of freezer paper the general height of the appliqué template. Draw the shape onto the paper. Accordion-fold the paper to the size of the piece to make multiple layers. Staple the folded layers together to keep them from slipping. Cut the shape from the freezer paper through all layers to make multiple pieces with one cut. Remove staple when ready to use. Remember, half of the templates will be reversed. Use this technique for templates that are symmetrical or for appliqué that needs some of the templates reversed.

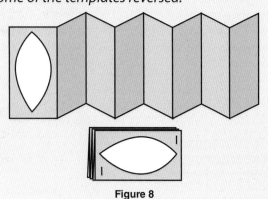

Figure 8

Number 2: Shiny Side Down— Wrong Side of Fabric

This technique is appropriate for appliqué shapes that should be reversed and for use with fusible web application discussed on page 12.

1. Create a reversed or mirror image by taping the appliqué design facedown on a light box or sunny window. Layer freezer paper shiny side down over the appliqué design. Trace around the appliqué template onto the dull side of the freezer paper.

2. Cut the actual shape from the paper. Do not add a seam allowance.

3. Iron the shiny side of the freezer-paper piece to the wrong side of the fabric. Using a sharp, hard pencil or stylus, trace around the template to crease the seam-allowance fold line. Cut the fabric around the shape, leaving a ¼" seam allowance.

4. Clip into the seam allowances almost to the creased line. Clip only on the inside curves and "V" areas, again referring to Figure 5—clip as little as possible.

5. Using a water-soluble glue stick, apply glue to seam allowance and the edge of the template. Finger-press the seam allowance over the edge of the paper. Move along the seam-allowance edge carefully to create smooth curves and crisp points, adding glue as needed. Remove any excess fabric at the "V"s as shown in Figure 9.

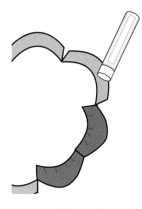

Figure 9

6. Place prepared pieces in a plastic bag to protect them until they are ready to use.

7. After the pieces have been stitched to the background, turn to the underside and cut away the background fabric under the appliqué pieces, leaving a ¼" seam allowance, referring to Figure 7. Remove the template.

Timely Tip

Use an appliqué or travel iron to press seam allowances onto the freezer paper.

Number 3: Easy Needle-Turn Technique
Shiny Side Down—Right Side of Fabric

This technique is a good introduction to needle-turn techniques. It allows the beginning or intermediate needleworker more control of the fabric, thread and needle.

1. Trace around the appliqué template onto the dull side of the freezer paper.

2. Cut the actual shape from the paper. Do not add a seam allowance.

3. Iron the freezer-paper piece to the right side of the fabric with the shiny side down. Cut the fabric around the shape, leaving a ¼" seam allowance. Turn to the wrong side. Using a sharp, hard pencil or stylus, trace around the template to crease the seam-allowance fold line as shown in Figure 10. This will take a little practice.

Figure 10

4. Clip into the seam allowances almost to the creased line. Clip only on the inside curves and "V" areas, again referring to Figure 5—clip as little as possible.

5. Place prepared pieces in a plastic bag to protect them until they are ready to use.

6. After the pieces have been stitched to the background, remove the freezer paper template and turn to the underside and cut away the background fabric under the appliqué pieces, leaving a ¼" seam allowance, referring to Figure 7.

Pressing Template Technique

This technique takes practice and is appropriate for most simple or larger appliqué shapes.

1. Pressing Templates: Begin with templates made from a thin cardboard, like manila file folders or heat-resistant plastic. Use heavily starched fabric. Place a pressing template, facedown, on the wrong side of the fabric. Using a sharp, hard pencil, (light-colored pencil on dark fabrics and dark-colored pencil on light fabrics) mark the outline of the shape on the fabric. Press hard enough to crease the fabric. When marking several pieces on the same fabric, leave at least ½" between pieces.

2. Cut the pieces from fabric, leaving a ¼" seam allowance outside the marked line.

3. Clip into the seam allowances almost to the stitching line. Only clip on inside curves or into "V" areas—clip as little as possible, again referring to Figure 5.

4. Place pressing template inside the marked line on the wrong side of the fabric.

5. Using a hot iron, press the seam allowance over the edge of the pressing template as for Freezer-Paper Technique No. 1. Continue all around the shape as shown in Figure 6. Move along the seam-allowance edge carefully to create smooth curves and crisp points.

6. Remove the template from the fabric as shown in Figure 11. The seam allowance will be folded down, and you should see a crisp line at the fold.

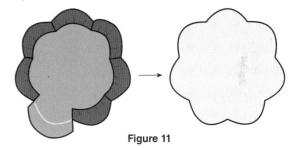

Figure 11

7. Turn the shape over and press firmly with the iron. Take care that you do not disturb the fold.

8. Use the piece immediately or baste the seam allowance under for future use. Store in plastic bags for protection until use.

Facing Techniques

These are easy techniques appropriate for simple shapes and for adding the illusion of dimension or stuffing when desired.

Facing Fabrics: For flat appliqué, use nylon tulle or pre-washed, lightweight, non-woven, non-fusible interfacing, or other washable, sheer fabric. When creating dimensional shapes, face with the same fabric as used for the appliqué piece.

Flat Technique

1. Lightly mark around the outline of a template onto the wrong side of the sheer facing fabric. Cut a small slit in the center of this marked fabric.

2. Place the facing fabric, right sides together, with the appliqué fabric.

3. Machine-stitch completely around the drawn outline using a small stitch and thread matching the appliqué fabric as shown in Figure 12. Cut around the outside of the stitching line, leaving a ⅛" seam allowance.

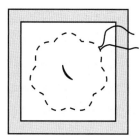

Figure 12

4. Clip the inward curves almost to the stitching, again referring to Figure 5.

5. Using your fingers or a hemostat, turn the appliqué piece to the right side through the small opening in the facing fabric, Figure 13.

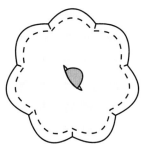

Figure 13

6. Smooth the seams to the shape of the piece and press lightly with an iron.

Timely Tip

After you have stitched the appliqué in place and you are sure of the placement, cut the background fabric and the facing from under the applied piece, referring to Figure 7.

Why?

Reason 1: *By cutting the background fabric away you will allow the batting to fill the area under the appliqué—no more flat appliqué!*

Reason 2: *It will be easier to quilt the appliqué designs.*

Dimensional Technique
The dimensional technique uses the same process as the flat facing technique. However, use the appliqué fabric as the facing fabric and stitch lines inside the shape to give the appliqué piece dimension.

1. Lightly mark around the outline of a template onto the wrong side of the appliqué facing fabric. Cut a small slit in the center of this marked fabric.

2. Place the facing fabric right sides together with appliqué fabric.

3. Machine-stitch completely around the drawn outline using a small stitch and thread matching the appliqué fabric. Cut around the outside of the stitching line, leaving a ⅛" seam allowance.

4. Clip the inward curves almost to the stitching.

5. Using your fingers or a hemostat, turn the appliqué piece to the right side through the small opening in the facing fabric.

6. Smooth the seams to the shape of the piece and press lightly with an iron.

7. To create a dimensional shape, place wrong side down on the background fabric and stitch lines within the shape to give it dimension. ***Note:*** *Refer to the Persian Flower quilt on page 48.*

Fusible-Web Techniques
The fusible-web technique allows you to appliqué even very complicated shapes quickly. This method eliminates the need to fold under a seam allowance. Do not add seam allowances when calculating fabric requirements or cutting the shapes from fabric.

Fabric-fusing products are sold by the yard, in packages or on rolls in fabric stores. These paper-backed products are available in various weights. Read and follow the manufacturer's instructions for application. Keep the original instructions with any leftover product.

Instructions differ from manufacturer to manufacturer and according to the thickness or weight of the webbing. Choose lighter-weight fusing materials if you plan to stitch through them.

Timely Tips

1. Before committing to a large or important project using a fusing method, you should test the fusing materials on your fabrics. Make sure the feel of the fused fabrics is what you desire.

2. Lightweight webbing will require stitching after being fused. Heavyweight webbing is usually permanent and very stiff after ironing in place and is best for banners, not quilts.

Using Fusing Products

Caution: Unless your project is designed for fusible webbing, you will, most likely, need to create a mirror image of the pattern using the No. 2 freezer-paper technique on page 10, or make sure you turn the "face" of each piece down toward the wrong side of the fabric, again referring to Figure 4.

Whole-Design Fusing

This technique is best for designs with layering within the design.

1. Label the right side of the template (or use the No. 2 freezer-paper technique on page 10 to create a reversed template).

2. Place the template right side down on the paper side of the webbing. Trace all the pieces needed from the same fabric about ½" apart on the paper side of the fusible, referring to Figure 14.

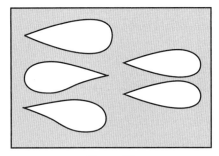

Figure 14

3. Place the fusible product paper side up on the wrong side of the fabric. Using the manufacturer's instructions, tack the product onto the fabric by touching the iron to the backing paper here and there. Then press from the center toward the edges. Caution: Do not distort the shape of the appliqué.

4. Cut out each shape on the outside of the traced line. Do not remove the paper backing yet.

5. Place a full-size appliqué pattern beneath a clear, non-stick pressing sheet. Layer the appliqué pieces right side up on the pressing sheet following the pattern. Remove paper backing from pieces. Lightly fuse the pieces together. Allow them to cool. Remove the layered and "basted" appliqué design from the pressing sheet; position and fuse on the appliqué background.

6. Finish the edge of the appliqués with your choice of stitching.

Window-Pane Technique

This technique leaves a softer look and feel to the fused appliqué. It also reduces the stiffness of shapes layered and fused on top of one another.

1. Trace each shape right side down onto the paper backing of the webbing (or use freezer-paper tech-

nique No. 2 on page 10 to created reversed templates). Do not add seam allowance. (Figure 15A)

2. Carefully trim inside each shape, leaving ⅛"–¼" inside the traced line as shown in Figure 15B and discard inside shape. Cut out shape approximately ¼" outside traced line (Figure 15C).

3. Place the fusible product paper side up on the wrong side of the fabric. Tack the product onto the fabric by touching the iron to the backing here and there; press window pane to fabric. Caution: Do not distort the shape of the appliqué. Do not remove the paper backing (Figure 15D).

4. Cut each shape from the fused fabric along traced outlines (Figure 15E). Remove the paper backing only when you are ready to use a piece.

6. Arrange appliqué pieces on the right side of the background fabric using an overlay or the whole-design fusing method, and fuse in place using the manufacturer's instructions.

Template

15A

15B

15C

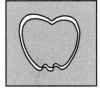

15D

15E

Figure 15

Timely Tips

1. To protect your ironing board and iron from fabric-fusing products, place a piece of typing paper between the fusible pieces and the iron and ironing board. Clear, non-stick pressing sheets are also available to be used on the ironing board.

2. A liquid-stitch product can be used to seal fabric edges. Use it to quickly baste an appliqué shape to the background for any hand or machine technique.

3. Use overlay transparency technique on page 19, for accurate placement of design elements.

A Special Technique: Shadow Appliqué

Shadow appliqué uses a semi-transparent or sheer fabric over raw-edge appliqué pieces. A row of stitching around each piece protects the edges by trapping them between the background layer and the sheer fabric. See Tropical Oasis on page 41.

Because there is an over-laid sheer fabric, you should choose brighter and higher contrasting fabrics for the appliqués.

1. Use a light-fusing procedure, like the window-pane technique, to prepare and secure the appliqué pieces to the background fabric.

2. Cut a piece of the sheer fabric the same size as the background fabric. Cover the background fabric with the sheer fabric as shown in Figure 16. Baste around edges of background and sheer fabrics.

Figure 16

3. Make decorative, running or quilting stitches around the appliqué pieces through all layers. Remove basting after stitching quilt blocks together.

Timely Tip

In some circumstances, the complete project can be layered for quilting before the stitches are made over the sheer fabric. In this way, the design can be completely decorated, stitched down and quilted all at the same time!

Finer Points in Appliqué Technique

Appliqué is very forgiving as a technique, but there are a few firm guidelines to follow—circles should be smooth, pointed leaves should remain pointed and stems and vines should be of even width and appear to move gracefully.

The good thing about these guidelines is that even a beginner can quickly learn the skills it takes to follow them.

Pointed Leaves—With Seam Allowance

Using either the Freezer Paper or Pressing Templates technique, press the seam allowance over the paper as shown in Figure 17.

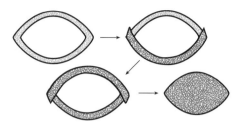

Figure 17

Don't cut excess fabric tag at the ends of the leaf. Instead, roll this seam-allowance fabric tag under the leaf just before you stitch it down.

Perfect Circles—With Seam Allowance

Method 1

Pin freezer-paper circle, shiny side up, to wrong side of circle fabric; trim seam allowance to ⅛". Carefully press the allowance over the freezer paper with a hot iron, creating small pleats as shown in Figure 18.

Figure 18

Method 2

Stitch ⅛" around outside edge of fabric circle. Place a paper template in center of circle and draw up the fabric, yo-yo style, around the template as shown in Figure 19. Make a knot; press. The paper template is removed after the circle is stitched down.

Figure 19

Method 3

This method is good for small circles. Stitch ⅛" around the outside edge of circle of fabric. Put a circle of either non-woven interfacing or 100 percent cotton fabric in the center of the circle of fabric and draw up the fabric, yo-yo style, around the template. Make a knot; press. The insert is not removed after the circle is stitched down.

Stacked Designs

Many appliqué pieces will have layers of design built up over just one foundation piece. All of the flowers in the Cornucopia With Strawberries quilt, page 52, have at least one center circle layered over each flower. To complete, place center circle on flower and appliqué in place. Place a small center on a medium center and appliqué in place as shown in Figure 20; appliqué flower to background.

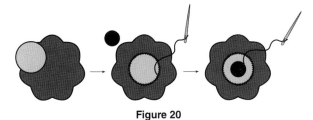

Figure 20

Stems & Vines

It's easy to make flowing, flat stems and vines with bias bars and tape makers. Yards and yards of even-width bias can be made in minutes and saved until needed.

Making Bias Strips

1. Fold a corner of fabric over to make a 45-degree angle; finger-press fold.

2. Open fabric and cut along fold as shown in Figure 21.

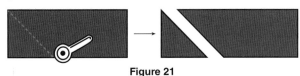

Figure 21

3. Follow the bias bar and bias tube manufacturer's guidelines for the width of strip you will need for the finished bias width. Cut strips the desired width using first cut edge as a guide as shown in Figure 22.

Figure 22

Timely Tip

You will need to experiment with the width of fabric. The width of your sewing-machine foot and your stitching habits will ultimately determine the width of strips you will need to cut.

4. Join the strips to form a longer strip, by sewing the short ends together as shown in Figure 23.

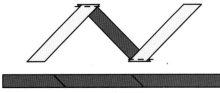

Figure 23

Using Bias Bars

Bias bars come in many widths from ⅛"–1". Bias tubes are sewn from bias strips of fabric.

1. Press the bias strip in half lengthwise with wrong sides together as shown in Figure 24A.

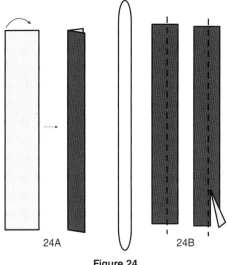

24A   24B

Figure 24

2. Make a line of machine stitching two or three threads wider than the bias bar to create a bias tube, again referring to Figure 24B.

3. Trim excess fabric close to stitching.

4. Place bias bar into tube; slip seam line around to centered on bar as shown in Figure 25, pressing seam open.

5. Spray-starch the front of the fabric and press with an iron. Slip the bar through the fabric tube and continue pressing.

6. Wrap the finished bias tube around an old spool or a piece of cardboard until you are ready to use it as shown in Figure 26.

Figure 26   **Figure 25**

Using the Bias Tape Maker

Bias tape makers are tools that fold bias strips into usable, folded bias tapes. Bias tape makers come in many different widths.

1. Feed a bias strip into the wide end of a complementary width tape maker. Push fabric through with a pin if necessary as shown in Figure 27.

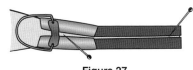

Figure 27

2. Pin the end to the ironing board. Pull tape maker along the bias strip. Press folded bias tape as it emerges from the narrow end of the tape maker.

3. Wrap finished bias tape around an old spool or a piece of cardboard until you are ready to use it, referring to Figure 26.

Using Bias Tubes & Tapes

Prepared bias tubes and tapes are flexible and are capable of being coaxed into delightful, flowing curves for stems and vines.

Measure the amount of stems or vines needed for the appliqué design and cut from the prepared bias tubing or tape. Baste into place and stitch down using an invisible stitch.

Timely Tip

As you hand-stitch stems and vines, sew inside curves first. This allows any fullness in the bias to expand on the opposite side. Begin by stitching on an inside curve. Pass needle under the bias when the direction in the curve changes and continue stitching on the opposite side along inner curve as shown in Figure 28. Finish stem by stitching outer curves in same manner.

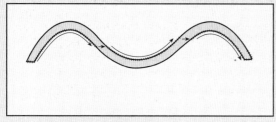

Figure 28

Reverse Appliqué

Reverse appliqué is a quick and easy way to get detail in a design. The freezer-paper technique is an efficient way to do reverse appliqué. I find it quick and sure.

1. Prepare a reversed template, referring to step 1 of freezer-paper technique No. 2 on page 10.

2. Pin freezer-paper template shiny side up on wrong side of fabric. Cut fabric about ¼" from outside edge of pattern as shown in Figure 29. Cut slits into edges along inner curves.

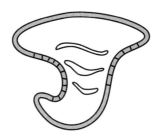
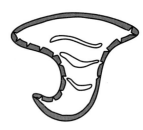

Figure 29 **Figure 30**

3. Press edges of fabric onto freezer paper with tip of iron, referring to Figure 30 and freezer-paper technique No. 1, page 9.

4. Cut slit in center open areas of pattern about ⅛"– ¼" from drawn edge; press edge of fabric in open areas onto freezer paper as shown in Figure 31.

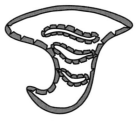

Figure 31 **Figure 32**

5. Place different piece of fabric, right side down, on freezer paper centered over opening as shown in Figure 32; iron, pin or baste in place.

6. Appliqué-stitch inner edges in place on fabric square using an Invisible Stitch, referring to Figure 33. Carefully remove freezer paper after trimming underlay fabric approximately ¼" away from stitching.

Figure 33

Appliqué Stitches

There are many different stitches possible for both hand and machine appliqué. Read over the various techniques, and then choose the ones that most appeal to your needs and projects.

Utility Hand Stitches

There are several advantages to hand appliqué. It can be relaxing, fun and it's portable. One only needs a sharp needle, fine thread, a thimble and some fabric.

There are three common styles of utility hand stitches for appliqué over a folded edge—the invisible stitch, the whipstitch and the topstitch. In each technique the thread pulls the appliqué and background fabrics together in a secure bond.

Invisible Stitch Over Turned Edge

The invisible stitch (Figure 34) is made at ⅛"
maximum intervals through the rolled edge fold of
the seam allowance and should not be seen on the
appliqué or background fabric.

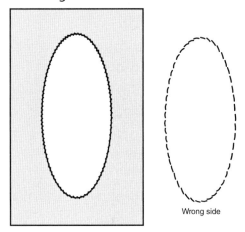

Figure 34

Push needle through seam-allowance fold from
back side; pull needle completely through fold.
Next, push needle through the background fabric
even with place where thread is; advance the
needle through the seam-allowance fold about
⅟₁₆"–⅛" away from first stitch, referring to Figure 35.
A little tug after each stitch secures the thread.

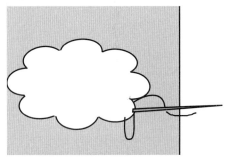

Figure 35

Today this is the stitch most commonly preferred
by quilters making heirloom-quality appliqué quilts
and takes a little practice to perfect.

Whipstitch Over Turned Edge

The whipstitch is made at ⅛" maximum intervals
through the bottom and top of the seam allowance
as shown in Figure 36. Because this stitch secures
the appliqué piece through two layers (Figure 37),
it creates a stronger bond with the background
fabric than does the invisible stitch. This stitch helps
protect the seam-allowance fold from wear. For this
reason, it is a good choice for appliqué quilts that
are expected to see much use.

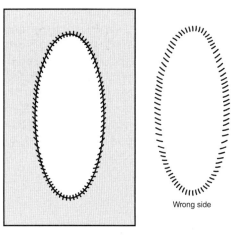

Wrong side

Figure 36

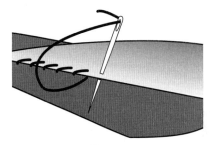

Figure 37

Topstitch Over Turned Edge

This utility stitch is quicker than either the invisible
or whipstitch. The stitch is made at ⅛"–¼" intervals
through the bottom and top of the seam allowance about ⅟₁₆" from the fold as shown in Figure
38. Because this stitch secures the appliqué piece
through two layers, it creates a strong bond with
the background fabric. The appearance of the
stitch is also somewhat decorative and is an excel-
lent choice for
contemporary
hand appliqué.
Topstitch use
for appliqué
was revived by
Jean Ray Laury
in the mid-1950s
on Tom's Quilt.
This particular
quilt has had a
significant influ-
ence on contem-
porary appliqué
quiltmaking.

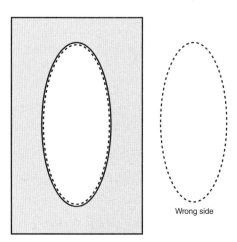

Wrong side

Figure 38

House of White Birches, Berne, Indiana 46711   Clotilde.com

Broderie Perse Over Raw Edge

This very old appliqué technique is still useful. Flora, fauna or objects are first cut from printed fabric—originally chintz. The pieces have a thin band of glue placed on the raw fabric edge. Then the pieces are arranged on the background fabric using a collage technique. Finally, they are stitched to the background using a very small, close, buttonhole-style stitch. A fine matching thread is used for each piece (Figure 39).

Figure 39

Utility-Machine Stitches

Another significant influence on quilts today is the use of the sewing machine for appliqué. One would be wrong to think that sewing machines were commonly used for appliqué only with the arrival of the zigzag-stitch machine. Many wonderful mid-to-late 19th-century quilts have the appliqué pieces topstitched by machine! Machine appliqué is faster and stronger than hand appliqué and for many quilters, it is a reasonable alternative to handwork.

Read your sewing-machine manual to analyze the kinds of stitches your sewing machine can make. You will need to experiment with stitch style, thread tension, length and width of stitch for the best possible results. A machine-appliqué foot, with an open under-channel, is used for most of these stitches. Thread type and color are critical in machine appliqué—on the top and in the bobbin—particularly when thread tension is problematic. Keep a note pad handy to record particularly useful combinations of width and length.

Timely Tip

The Broderie Perse technique is easily replicated by machine using a fine thread and a very small buttonhole stitch. Use either glue, starch or the Window-Pane fusing technique to secure the raw edge. In Tropical Oasis, I've used a liquid-stitch product to seal the edge.

Topstitch Over Turned Edge

Any sewing machine can topstitch appliqué pieces to the background fabric, again referring to Figure 38. It is a very strong stitch. Use with a turned-under seam allowance.

Blind Hem Stitch Over Turned Edge

The machine blind-hem stitch (Figure 40) can give the look of invisible hand appliqué.

Thread color and the relationship between the appliqué edge and needle are critical. Experiment with stitch width, length and type of thread best suited for the results you want.

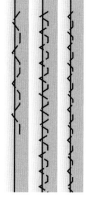

Figure 40

Hidden Zigzag Stitch Over Turned Edge

When using a short stitch length and width, a zigzag stitch gives the appearance of a whipped stitched edge (Figure 41). Thread color and the relationship between the appliqué edge and needle are critical.

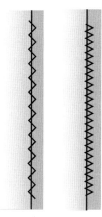

Figure 41

Decorative Stitches— Hand & Machine

Many decorative machine stitches are appropriate to use over or next to the folded edge in appliqué. You will want to experiment with several—be creative!

Blanket Stitch

A small, close blanket stitch gives the appearance of the traditional Broderie-Perse hand-stitch technique for finishing an unturned appliqué edge (Figure 42).

A larger hand-stitched blanket stitch, over a turned-edge appliqué technique, gives the look of current folk art-style appliqué and the appliqué from the 1920s and 1930s (Figure 43).

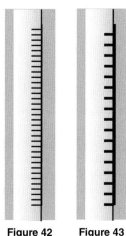

Figure 42   **Figure 43**

Chain & Backstitch Over or Beside Turned Edge

A chain or backstitch can outline an appliqué design element and add interesting detail.

Experiment with additional machine decorative stitches. Be inventive! These stitches can also be added by hand or machine for special interest (Figure 44).

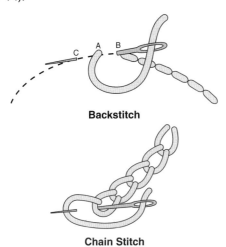

Backstitch

Chain Stitch

Figure 44

Satin Stitch Over Raw Edge

The satin stitch can be used as a utility and a decorative stitch all at the same time. The satin stitch (Figure 45) is a heavy-duty utility stitch for appliqué. This stitch gives a strong decorative outline to the design. It is the slowest of the machine techniques.

Use an open-channel appliqué foot.

Figure 45

Centering & Arranging the Pieces for Appliqué

Planning the placement of the design is a common problem in appliqué quilts. For this reason I prefer to use and teach the techniques I've outlined. With each of these techniques the appliqué pieces are exactly the same size as they will be when they are applied. We can layer the design elements easily knowing their exact relationship to each other. Those of you who are computer literate know the old acronym—WYSIWYG, What You See Is What You Get—I also believe that applies to preparing, planning and arranging your appliqué pieces.

1. Using the actual templates, or original design, very lightly draw an outline of the exact finished block onto plastic overlay material. Make sure to include any centering lines and symbols (Figure 46).

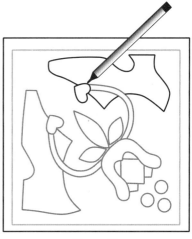

Figure 46

2. Lightly draw or press centering lines on the background blocks. If your design is a simple one, making diagonal lines across the block will probably be sufficient. The more complicated the appliqué design, the more guidelines you will likely need as shown in Figure 47.

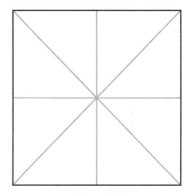

Figure 47

3. Center, and then pin the overlay plastic to the background fabric.

4. Arrange the appliqué pieces on the background fabric, under the plastic, paying attention to the order in which the pieces of the design will need to be applied. Think of the placement order like this: Whatever goes behind something else is applied

Timely Tip

1. Always stop your needle in the down, dropped position when you machine appliqué.

2. When applying curved pieces you will drop the needle, pivot the fabric around the needle and stitch. Remember to: drop, pivot, stitch; drop, pivot, stitch; repeat. Read your sewing-machine manual for detailed satin-stitch information.

3. Always slow down at curves and points!

first—for example, stems, leaves and then the flowers as shown in Figure 48.

Figure 48

Basting

Teacher, must we baste? Yes, and not just because I say so. You baste because you'll avoid losing parts of the design before they are applied and pieces aren't left out of the design in error. Placement and stitching-order mistakes are quickly seen and corrected when the piece is completely basted on the background fabric.

Timely Tip

After the design is basted in place, hold it up in front of a mirror. Design errors and errors in contrast and placement become immediately evident.

Basting With Pins & Glue Sticks or Stitchless Sewing Liquids

Using straight pins or glue-like products for basting is quick and easy. They can, temporarily, keep the elements of the appliqué design where you have planned and arranged them.

Timely Tip

To avoid catching the sewing thread on the head and point of the straight pin, place the basting pins on the underside of the background fabric. The pins hold the appliqué piece to the background fabric, and you can still see them enough to escape grabbing one in the palm of your hand.

Basting by Hand & Machine

Basting by hand or machine is ideal for very complex designs. A few large stitches through the appliqué design will keep the pieces in place longer and with fewer problems than either pin or glue-stick basting. Remove the basting threads when you are finished.

To baste multiple layers of a design when using fusible web, refer to whole design fusing on page 13.

Finishing the Quilt

Preparing the Quilt Top

When the center of the quilt top has been given a final pressing, prepare it for finishing by making sure all corners and sides are straight and square. The top and bottom of the piece should be the same measurement and the side measurements should match. Trim with rotary tools, if necessary, making sure to leave a ¼" seam allowance beyond all pieced points.

Borders

Cutting Border Strips

1. Cut border fabric to correspond to top and bottom quilt measurements as shown in Figure 49.

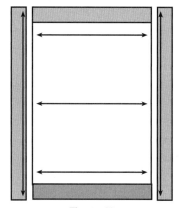

Figure 49

2. Pin border strips to the quilt at the ends and in the center. Sew borders to the quilt center.

3. Re-measure each side of the quilt, including borders and cut the side border strips to this measurement.

4. Pin borders to the sides of the quilt, at the ends and in the middle.

5. Sew borders to quilt.

6. For additional borders, repeat steps 1–5.

Borders with Corner Squares
1. Cut border strips to the top and bottom measurement.

2. Sew borders to quilt top. Press seams toward borders.

3. Cut border fabric to the true, original measurement of the sides of the quilt top, including seam allowances.

4. Cut four squares of fabric using the width of the border fabric measurement. For example, a 3"-wide border strip will need a 3" x 3" square.

5. Stitch the squares to the ends of the side borders as shown in Figure 50. Finger-press seams toward border strips.

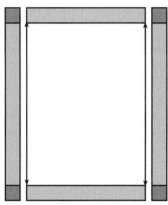
Figure 50

6. Sew the pieced borders to the sides of the quilt top matching the seams at the corner blocks.

Marking the Quilt
1. Plan quilting designs and method of quilting (by hand or machine) before layering backing, batting and quilt top.

2. Mark the quilting lines on the right side of quilt top, using a removable marking pencil, pen, or other quilt-marking tool. Test all marking tools before using on your quilt. Follow manufacturer's instructions for removing markings.

Batting & Backing
We have indicated the amount of fabric and batting required for each pattern. Use an appropriate batting for the end use of the quilt. Read manufacturer's specifications for the amount of quilting required, washing and general use.

Layering the Quilt
Cut batting and backing larger than the quilt top, about 2" wider than the top on all sides for hand quilting and 4" wider on all sides if long-arm quilting. Place backing wrong side up on a flat surface. Place batting on top of this, matching outer edges.

It is a good idea to remove batting from its packaging a day in advance and open it out full size. This will help the batting to lie flat and "relax."

Center the quilt top with right side up on top of the batting.

Basting the Layers
The layers of the quilt are basted either by thread or with safety pins before quilting.

For thread basting, pin backing, batting and quilt top together. Baste with long stitches, starting at the center of the quilt and working toward the outside of the quilt. Create a number of long diagonal lines of stitching.

For pin basting, pin backing, batting and quilt top together at 6" intervals. Start in the center and work toward the outside of the quilt. Avoid placing pins in prospective quilting lines.

Do not trim excess backing or batting after basting.

Quilting
Quilting can be done by hand or machine. I often machine-quilt long lines in the ditch and hand-quilt around the appliqué where it will show. Start quilting in the center and work toward the outside edges.

Hand Quilting
To quilt by hand, place the basted quilt in a quilting hoop or frame. Using a small needle (betweens in sizes Nos. 7–12) and quilting thread, make small, even running stitches along the quilting lines. Hand quilting for pieced projects often follows ¼" outside the seam. Hand quilting for appliqué projects follows the appliqué edge, about ¹⁄₁₆" outside the design. A second line of quilting is usually placed ¼" from the appliqué.

Machine Quilting—Feed Dogs Up
The feed dogs control the forward and backward motion of the quilt through the sewing machine.

To quilt by machine, use a fine, transparent nylon thread or 100 percent cotton machine thread for the top. Use cotton or cotton-covered polyester in the bobbin. Never use nylon thread in your bobbin.

An even-feed foot is a good investment if you are going to machine-quilt because it feeds the top and bottom layers through the machine evenly and helps prevent puckers.

Machine Quilting—Feed Dogs Down
This method is often called "hand-guided" or "free-motion" machine quilting. With this technique you will need a sewing-machine darning foot.

Place the darning foot on your sewing machine. If properly placed, the foot will not touch the machine footplate when it is in the down position.

Thread the sewing machine for machine quilting. Hand-guide the basted quilt under the darning foot through the same steps used in "feed dogs up" machine quilting. The only difference is that you control the forward movement of fabric along the quilting pattern. This takes practice to achieve the steadiness and speed control to obtain uniform-size stitches.

French-Fold Binding
Place the quilt on a flat surface and trim backing and batting even with the quilt-top edge. Measure around the quilt. Cut and join binding strips to that length. Binding width can be 2"–2½" depending on personal choice.

Next, press the strip in half lengthwise with wrong sides together. Open the fold and make a long diagonal cut across the bias as shown in Figure 51.

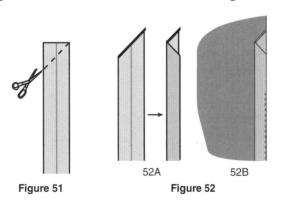

Figure 51   Figure 52

Fold down a ¼" seam along the bias edge. Re-fold strip lengthwise as shown in Figure 52A, and apply binding along edge of back of quilted top using a ¼" seam allowance as shown in Figure 52B.

At the corners, fold binding at a complete right angle to the stitching. Drop the needle and pivot

around the dropped needle. Continue stitching around the quilt and completing the corners as shown in Figure 53. This right-angle corner tuck will create a full mitered corner when turned to the other side and stitched down.

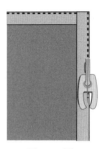

Figure 53   Figure 54

To finish the end of the binding, tuck the raw end into the bias cut at the beginning of the binding and finish sewing as shown in Figure 54.

Turn binding to the other side of the quilt and stitch down with a hidden slipstitch by hand or a machine-hemming stitch. Close the mitered corner tuck with a few additional hand stitches.

Making a Label for Your Quilt
Make a separate label for your quilt from muslin or another light fabric. Type, embroider or use a permanent fine-tip marker for the lettering. Include the name of the quilt, the name of the quilter(s), the date and any other pertinent information on the label as shown in Figure 55. Turn the edges to the wrong side and hand-stitch to the back of the quilt at bottom right corner.

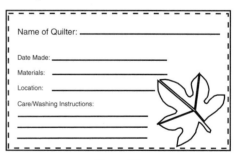

Figure 55

Timely Tip
Use the Facing Technique, pages 11 and 12, to quickly turn the edges of your quilt labels.

Adapting These Designs

How to Reduce or Enlarge the Designs

You might want to enlarge or reduce the sizes of the appliqué designs in this book. Most communities offer an abundance of self-serve photocopy or duplicating service shops. The percentages suggested are those I have found useful and available on local machines. Because you will be working within the limits of your available copy machines you may need to experiment with the percentages.

Assume you have an 8" design. The suggested percentages below will give you a comfortable margin of background fabric around the design. Some of us like to crowd the design right up to the seam allowance and some of us like to float the design on a bigger background. Test the sizes and designs before committing to a large project.

Reductions:

75% of page original = 6" design
50% of page original = 4" design

Enlargements:

125% of page original = 10" design
150% of page original = 12" design
175% of page original = 14" design
200% of page original = 16" design ❖

Name of Quilter:

Date Made:

Materials:

Location:

Care/Washing Instructions:

House of White Birches, Berne, Indiana 46711 Clotilde.com

Square Dance

Four appliquéd blocks dance around the center squares with 44 spinning Pinwheel blocks surrounding the dancing feet.

Square Dance
10" x 10" Block
Make 4

Pinwheel
2" x 2" Block
Make 44

Timely Tip

Use a paper-foundation technique to create accurate half-square triangles for the Pinwheel blocks. A diagram for creating these blocks is provided.

Project Specifications
Quilt Size: 32" x 32"
Block Sizes: 10" x 10", 2" x 2",
Number of Blocks: 4, 44

Materials Needed
- Assorted light and dark fabric scraps for Pinwheel blocks
- Black, red, violet and gold scraps for flowers and hearts
- ⅛ yard brown fabric for man's shoes
- ⅛ yard brown fabric for woman's shoes
- ¼ yard green fabric for leaves and stems
- ½ yard white/black fabric for background squares
- ⅞ yard red/black fabric for borders and binding
- Backing 40" x 40"
- Batting 40" x 40"
- All-purpose thread to match fabrics
- Freezer paper
- Copy paper
- Basic sewing tools and supplies

Pattern
Dancing Shoes

Cutting
1. Cut four 10½" x 10½" A background squares from the white/black background fabric.

2. Cut two 4½" x 24½" B strips and four 4½" x 32½" C strips red/black print for second border.

3. Cut four 2¼" by fabric width strips red/black print for binding.

4. Cut five bias strips from green fabric. Create 42" bias tape ¼" wide for stems, referring to page 15.

Appliqué Blocks
1. Create the plastic overlay of the appliqué motif on page 27 and referring to page 19, eliminating the vine and the flower center when tracing. Trace these pieces onto freezer paper separately.

2. Cut four pieces of freezer paper 10" x 10". Trace the motif onto one square of the freezer paper.

3. Align the traced square with the remaining layers of freezer paper and staple together outside the design area as shown in Figure 1; cut out shapes through all layers to create four freezer-paper shapes of each appliqué piece.

Figure 1

4. Prepare the fabrics for appliqué using one of the freezer-paper techniques, referring to pages 9–11. *Note: You should have four similar sets of prepared pieces for the Square Dance blocks*

5. Add the vine and flower center shapes to the plastic overlay created in step 1. Pin the plastic overlay onto one A square; slip the prepared fabric pieces under the overlay for correct placement of pieces; baste or pin in place as shown in Figure 2. Repeat with all four background squares.

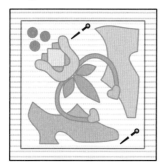

Figure 2

6. Check the placement of the overlapping parts, and then stitch the appliqué pieces in place with thread to match fabrics and small stitches.

7. When the block is complete, turn it over and trim the background fabric away from behind the applied fabrics, leaving a ¼" seam allowance.

8. Remove freezer papers to complete one Square Dance block.

9. Repeat steps 5–8 to complete a total of four Square Dance blocks.

Making the Pinwheel Borders

1. Make 22 copies of the 2-Block paper-piecing pattern (or 88 copies of the 2-Unit paper-piecing pattern for use with smaller scraps) for the Pinwheel blocks.

2. Layer a light and medium scrap with right sides together. Place a paper foundation over the wrong side of the layered pieces; pin in place as shown in Figure 3.

Figure 3

3. Increase the stitches per inch on your sewing machine. Sew on each dotted line in the direction of the arrow. Cut and trim the foundation along

Square Dance
Placement Diagram 32" x 32"

House of White Birches, Berne, Indiana 46711 Clotilde.com

the solid lines, as shown in Figure 4, to create half-square units.

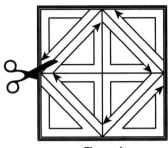

Figure 4

4. Peel off the paper, being careful not to disturb the stitching.

5. Open each half-square triangle unit and press the seam open. Trim the excess points of fabric as shown in Figure 5.

Figure 5

6. Repeat for all other half-square triangle units.

7. Select four half-square triangle units; join two to make a row, referring to Figure 6. Repeat to make two rows. Press seams in opposite directions. Join the two rows to complete a Pinwheel block. ***Note:*** *You may use four matching units or four different units to complete the pinwheels.*

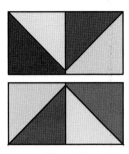

Figure 6

8. Repeat step 7 to complete a total of 44 Pinwheel blocks.

Finishing

1. Referring to the Placement Diagram for positioning, join two appliqué blocks to make a row; press. Repeat to make two rows. Join the rows to complete the pieced center, referring to the Placement Diagram.

2. Join 10 pinwheel units to make a side strip; press seams in one direction. Repeat to make two side strips.

3. Sew a side strip to opposite sides of the pieced center; press seams toward the pieced center.

4. Repeat step 2 to make two 12-unit pinwheel strips and sew to the top and bottom of the pieced center; press seams toward the pieced center.

5. Sew a B strip to opposite sides and C strips to the top and bottom of the pieced center; press seams toward strips.

6. Quilt and bind, referring to Finishing the Quilt on pages 20–23 to finish. ❖

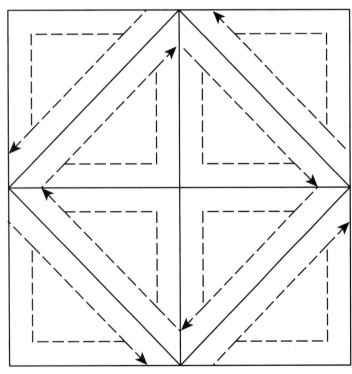

2-Block Paper-Piecing Pattern
Make 22 copies

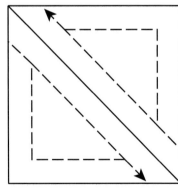

2-Unit Paper-Piecing Pattern
Make 88 copies

Timely Reminder
Make and use a plastic overlay for the design.
Review freezer-paper techniques on pages 9–11.

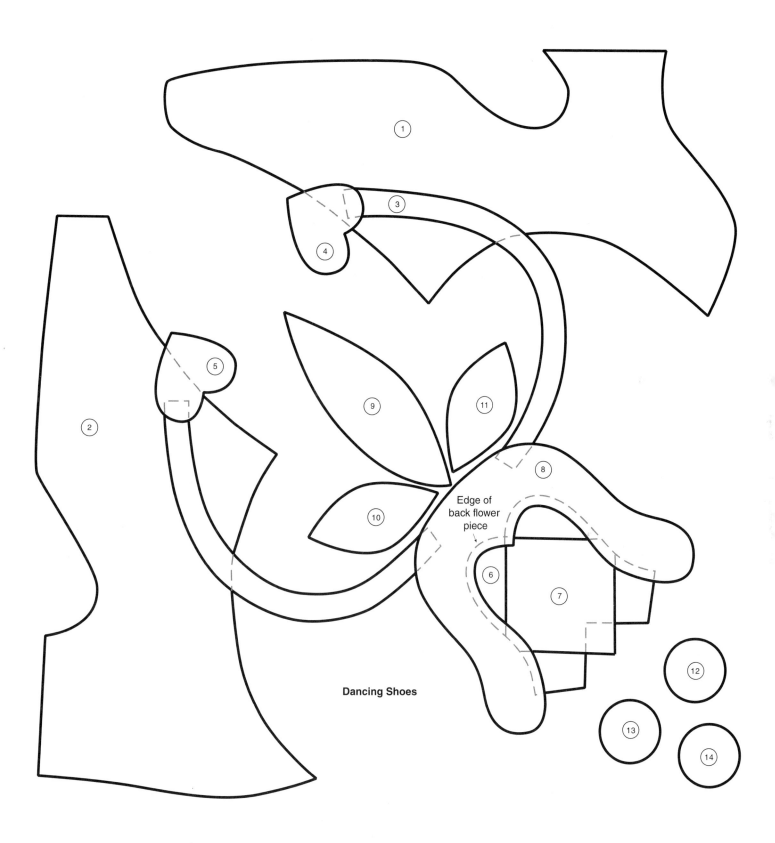

Edge of
back flower
piece

Dancing Shoes

House of White Birches, Berne, Indiana 46711   Clotilde.com

First Frost Table Runner

Shadow appliqué is as easy as a running stitch. Vivid autumn leaves cascade across the table runner as a hint of winter covers their brilliance.

Project Specifications
Skill Level: Beginner
Runner Size: 44" x 16"

Materials Needed
- Scrap magenta solid
- Assorted bright scraps
- ¼ yard coordinating stripe
- ¼ yard gold tonal
- ½ yard cream tonal
- ½ yard frosty/sparkly sheer fabric
- ½ yard magenta print
- Backing 52" x 24"
- Batting 52" x 24"
- All-purpose thread to match fabrics
- Quilting thread
- ½ yard 18"-wide fusible web
- Basic sewing tools and supplies

Cutting
1. Cut one 11½" x 39½" A rectangle cream tonal.

2. Cut two 1½" x 39½" B strips coordinating stripe.

3. Cut two 1½" by fabric width strips coordinating stripe; subcut strip into two 11½" D strips.

4. Cut four 1½" x 1½" C squares magenta solid.

5. Cut two 2" x 41½" E strips gold tonal.

6. Cut two 2" by fabric width strips gold tonal; subcut strips into two 16½" F strips.

7. Cut one 11½" x 39½" rectangle from the frosty/sparkly sheer fabric.

8. Cut four 2¼" by fabric width strips magenta print for binding.

9. Cut appliqué pieces from scraps as desired referring to Completing the Runner.

Completing the Runner
1. Pre-wash all fabrics to remove sizing. Dry and press if necessary.

2. Trace the various leaf and circle designs given onto the paper side of the fusible web as desired, leaving at least ¼" between pieces. *Note: There is a total of 14 leaves on the sample runner, but you may use as many as pleases you and in the colors you like.*

3. Cut out the paper shapes leaving a margin around each one. Fuse the shapes to the wrong side of the chosen fabrics for leaves and circles; cut out shapes on traced lines. Remove paper backing.

4. Place the A background rectangle right side up on your ironing surface; fuse the leaf and circle shapes in a pleasing arrangement.

5. Layer the sheer fabric rectangle over the right side of the fused A background rectangle, covering the appliqué pieces; carefully baste the layers together.

6. Sew B strips to opposite long sides of the appliquéd A rectangle; using a pressing cloth, press seams toward B strips. *Note: Some sheer fabrics will melt when exposed to heat from an iron. It is safer to use a pressing cloth to protect the sheer fabric layer.*

7. Sew a C square to each end of each D strip; press seams toward C.

8. Sew a C-D strip to opposite short ends of the appliquéd A rectangle; press as in step 6 with seams toward the C-D strips.

9. Sew E strips to opposite long sides and F strips to the short ends of the appliquéd A rectangle to complete the runner top; press with seams toward E and F strips as in step 6.

10. Sandwich the batting between the completed runner top and backing piece; baste layers together.

11. Using machine embroidery thread and a machine backstitch, sew around each leaf and circle.

12. Machine-quilt with a meandering pattern using thread to match the A rectangle; trim edges even when quilting is complete.

13. Bind edges, referring to Finishing the Quilt on pages 20–23. ❖

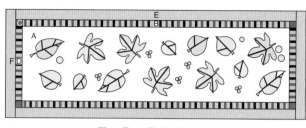

First Frost Table Runner
Placement Diagram 44" x 16"

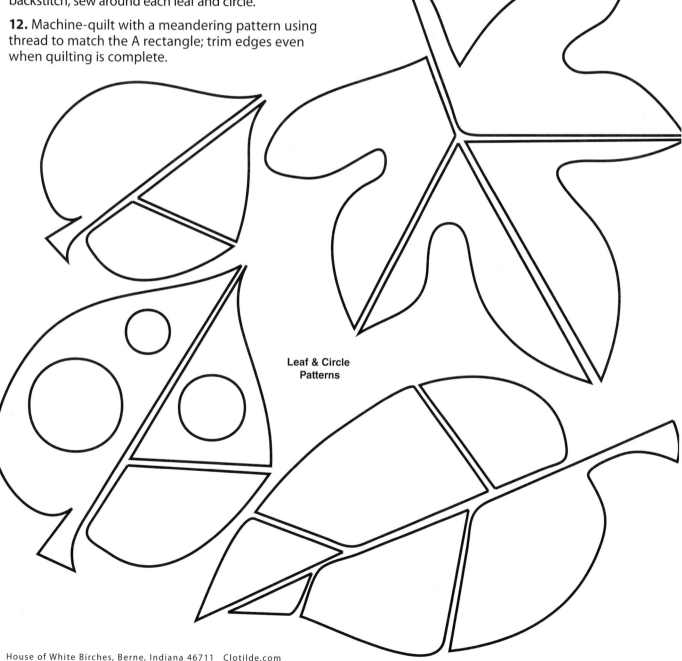

**Leaf & Circle
Patterns**

Forget-Me-Not

The Forget-Me-Not and Black-Eyed Susan floral designs in this wall quilt are represented by abstracted images from nature. This group of blocks is designed to work together—the curves and shapes are harmonious.

Project Specifications
Quilt Size: 32" x 32"
Block Size: 10" x 10" finished
Number of Blocks: 4

Materials Needed
- ⅛ yard blue print for flowers
- ¼ yard yellow/gold for flowers
- ⅜ yard green for leaves and stems
- ½ yard light background fabric
- ½ yard medium-light background fabric
- ⅝ yard blue check for first border and binding
- ⅝ yard large floral for second border
- 1⅛ yards backing and batting
- Neutral-color all-purpose thread
- Black 6-strand embroidery floss
- 1 yard paper-backed fusible webbing
- Basic sewing tools and supplies

Patterns
Large Flower
Small Flower
Leaf 1, 2 and 3
Flower Center 1 and 2

Project Notes
A blanket stitch was used to embellish around the edges of the simple appliqué shapes as well as on the borders. The quilt was hand- and machine-quilted.

Block 1
10" x 10" Block
Make 1

Block 2
10" x 10" Block
Make 1

Block 3
10" x 10" Block
Make 1

Block 4
10" x 10" Block
Make 1

Cutting

1. Cut two 12" x 12" A squares from the light background fabric and two 12" x 12" B squares from the medium-light background fabric.

2. Cut two 2½" x 20½" C strips and two 2½" x 24½" D strips blue check for first border.

3. Cut four 2¼" by fabric width strips blue check for binding.

4. Cut two 4½" x 24½" E strips and two 4½" x 32½" F strips large floral for second border.

Cutting Appliqué Pieces
For Block 1:
• 1 Large Flower, yellow/gold
• 1 Flower Center 2, brown check
• 2 Leaf 1, green
• 2 Leaf 2, green
• 10"–12" of ⅜"-wide bias strip, green

For Block 2
• 3 Small Flowers, blue print
• 3 Flower Center 1, gold
• 5 Leaf 2, green
• 1 Leaf 3, green
• 14"–18" of ⅜"-wide bias strip, green

For Block 3
• 4 Small Flowers, blue print
• 4 Flower Center 1, gold
• 4 Leaf 1, green
• 18" of ⅜"-wide bias strip, green

For Block 4:
• 1 Large Flower, yellow/gold
• 1 Flower Center 2, brown check
• 6 Leaf 1, green

Appliqué Blocks

1. Lightly draw a 10" x 10" square in the center of each A and B background square; draw diagonal lines from corner to corner and down the center of each side as shown in Figure 1.

2. Prepare the appliqué pieces using patterns given, referring to the Fusible-Web Techniques instructions on page 12.

3. Arrange the appliqué pieces on the background squares, referring to the block drawings for positioning.

4. When sure of placement, fuse pieces in place following manufacturer's directions.

5. Stitch edges of appliqué pieces using a blanket stitch, referring to Appliqué Stitches on pages 16–19.

6. Trim squares to 10½" x 10½" (¼" beyond the drawn line).

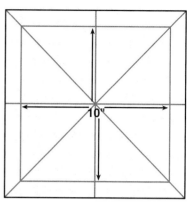

Figure 1

Finishing

1. Referring to the Placement Diagram for positioning, join the appliqué blocks to make two block rows; press. Join the rows to complete the pieced center.

2. Sew C border strips to sides of pieced center. Sew D strips to the top and bottom. Press seams toward C and D strips. Repeat with E and F large floral strips for second border to complete the top.

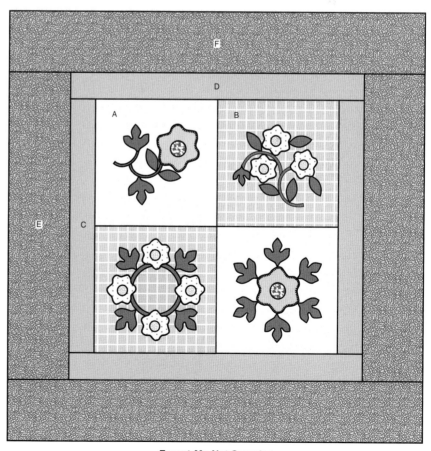

Forget-Me-Not Sampler
Placement Diagram 32" x 32"

House of White Birches, Berne, Indiana 46711 Clotilde.com

3. Quilt and bind, referring to Finishing the Quilt on pages 20–23 to finish, stitching a blanket stitch around edges of each block and between first and second border using 2 or 3 strands of black embroidery floss. ❖

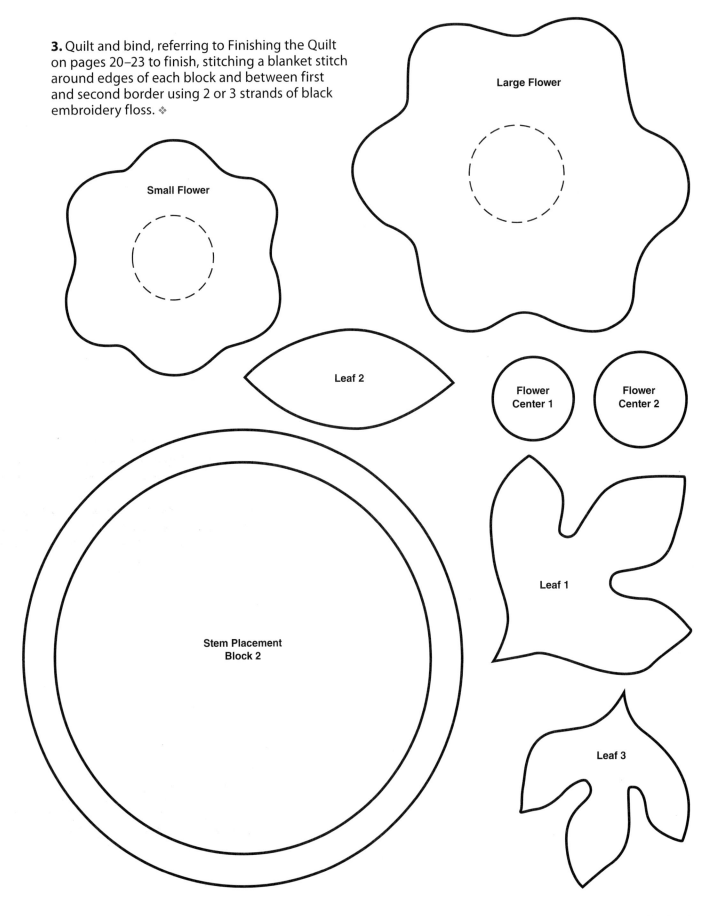

Large Flower

Small Flower

Leaf 2

Flower Center 1

Flower Center 2

Leaf 1

Stem Placement
Block 2

Leaf 3

Square Dance, page 24

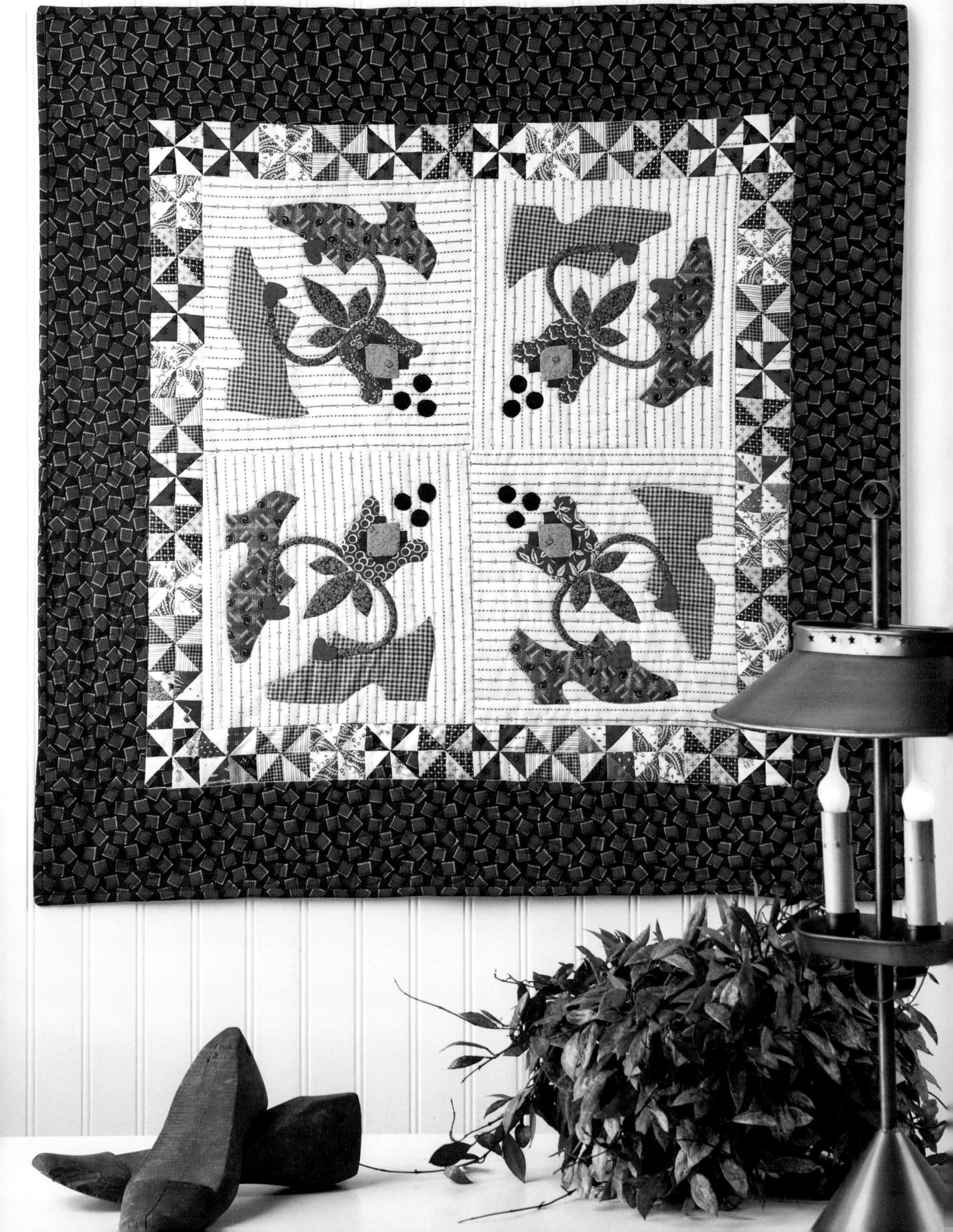

Persian Flower, page 48

Cornucopia with Strawberries, page 52

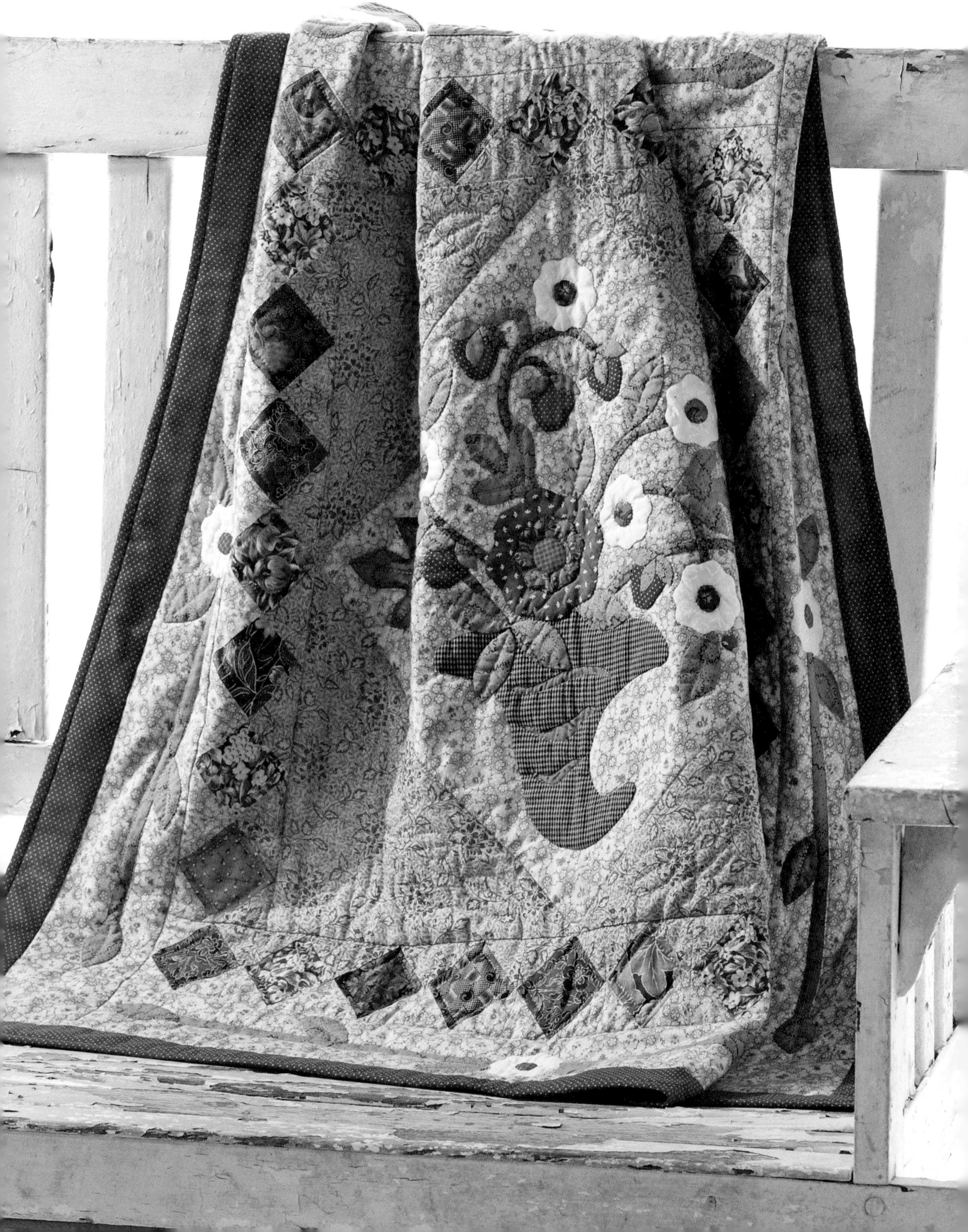

Tropical Oasis

Create your own tropical paradise with this brightly colored quilt
and learn how to do fusible and shadow appliqué at the same time.

Finished Size
Quilt Size: 32½" x 32½"

Materials Needed
- 4 (5½" x 5½") squares each vivid green and olive green fabrics
- 2 (5½" x 5½") squares each red/violet and blue fabrics
- 1 (5½" x 5½") square orange fabric
- Scraps red and yellow/orange fabric for appliqué
- ⅛ yard gold fabric for leaves
- ⅛ yard peach fabric for leaves
- ¼ yard polyester organdy for shadow appliquéd circles
- ½ yard green leaf fabric for accent border and appliqué
- 1¼ yards turquoise fabric for finishing triangles, border and binding
- Backing 40" x 40"
- Batting 40" x 40"
- All-purpose thread to match fabrics
- Machine-embroidery thread to match or contrast with appliqué fabrics
- ½ yard lightweight fusible webbing
- Basic sewing tools and supplies

Cutting
1. Cut two 2" x 21⅞" C strips and two 2" x 24⅞" D strips green leaf fabric.

2. Cut two 4½" x 24⅞" E strips and two 4½" x 32⅞" F strips turquoise fabric.

3. Cut one 8⅜" by fabric width strip turquoise fabric; subcut strip into two 8⅜" squares and two

4½" x 4½" squares. Cut the large squares on both diagonals to make eight large A triangles as shown in Figure 1. Cut the small squares in half on one diagonal to make four small B triangles, again referring to Figure 1.

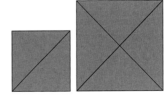

Figure 1

4. Cut four 2¼" by fabric width strips turquoise fabric for binding.

5. Cut two 5½" x 5½" squares organdy for shadow appliqué.

Timely Tip

When using a fusible-appliqué method, you can quilt and appliqué the fused pieces in place in one step.

House of White Birches, Berne, Indiana 46711   Clotilde.com

Appliquéd Leaves

1. Referring to Fusible-Web Techniques on page 12, trace the leaf designs given onto the paper side of the fusible web, referring to the Placement Diagram for number to cut; cut apart, leaving a margin around each one. ***Note:*** *The orange leaf combines two sections on one side of the leaf as shown in Figure 2.*

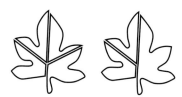

Figure 2

2. Trace a random number of circles on the remaining fusible web using the patterns given.

3. Fuse the shapes to the wrong side of the fabrics listed for each leaf and as desired for circles; cut out shapes on traced lines. Remove paper backing.

4. Arrange and fuse leaf sections and circles on the squares as desired.

5. Overlay the blue squares with the organdy squares; pin or baste in place.

Completing the Top

1. Arrange and join the fused squares with the vivid green squares and the small B and large A triangles in diagonal rows, referring to Figure 3; press seams in adjacent rows in opposite directions.

2. Join the rows to complete the pieced center; press seams open.

3. Sew C strips to opposite sides and D strips to the top and bottom of the pieced center; press seams open.

Timely Reminder

When using the fusible-appliqué technique, remember that the design will need to be reversed.

4. Sew E strips to opposite sides and F strips to the top and bottom of the pieced center; press seams open.

Figure 3

Tropical Oasis
Placement Diagram 32½" x 32½"

Finishing

1. Prepare the quilt top for quilting, referring to Finishing the Quilt on pages 20–23.

2. Using thread to match fabrics and a close satin stitch, machine-stitch around fused shapes through all layers to appliqué and quilt in one step.

3. Stitch close to edges of the appliquéd shapes through the organdy to attach the organdy to the appliquéd background square and quilt in one step.

4. Quilt a leaf design in the vivid green squares.

5. Quilt and bind edges, again referring to Finishing the Quilt on pages 20–23. ❖

Leaf & Circle
Patterns

"A" is for Apple

This little Apple project will get you started in appliqué! Choose one technique to start; you'll probably want to try all three just for fun!

Easy Needle-Turn Appliqué

Project Notes
The apple shape with leaves and stem will teach you most of what you need to know to tackle more difficult appliqué projects. Review the technique sections covering the techniques you want to learn. Then apply them to the variation you've chosen.

Finished Size
Quilt Size: 10" x 10"

Timely Tips

1. Look at the apple design page. There is a centering + on the apple. Make sure this + is on your plastic overlay sheet. It will help you center the design on the background fabric.

2. Before you start the leaves, re-read the information about the 'dog-ears!'

Materials Needed
- Scraps green fabrics for leaves and stem
- Scrap red fabric for letter A
- 1 (6½" x 6½") square background fabric
- 1 (4½" x 4½") square red fabric for apple
- 4 (2½" x 2½") squares background fabric for corner squares
- 4 (2½" x 6½") rectangles red fabric for borders
- Backing 14" x 14"
- Batting 14" x 14"
- 2¼" x 42" strip binding fabric

Pattern:
"A" is for Apple

Instructions
1. Prepare your appliqué design and fabric, referring to Easy Needle-Turn Technique on page 11.

2. Note the placement numbers on the Apple design. These show you which design element must be placed and sewn down first.

True Story: *A new student had made her first Sunbonnet Sue quilt, and she showed it to me. She had had such a good time sewing Sue that she had totally forgotten to first place Sue's feet and hands before her clothing and arm. Sue was footless and handless. She knew what she needed to do, but she hoped I might have a better solution. I didn't. She had to un-sew part of every Sue block in order to insert her feet and hands.*

3. Complete the appliqué, referring to Easy Needle-Turn Technique on page 11.

Timely Tip
Caution—most appliqué designs will not show you the order in which you must place the parts of the design. If this is the case, you must plan the order of placement very carefully.

4. Assemble the quilt as shown in Figure 1, adding borders and corner squares.

Figure 1

5. Layer the top, batting and backing and quilt as desired. Finish with binding and a label, referring to page 22.

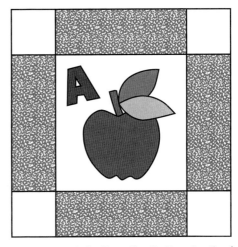

"A" is for Apple for Easy Needle-Turn Appliqué
Placement Diagram 10" x 10"

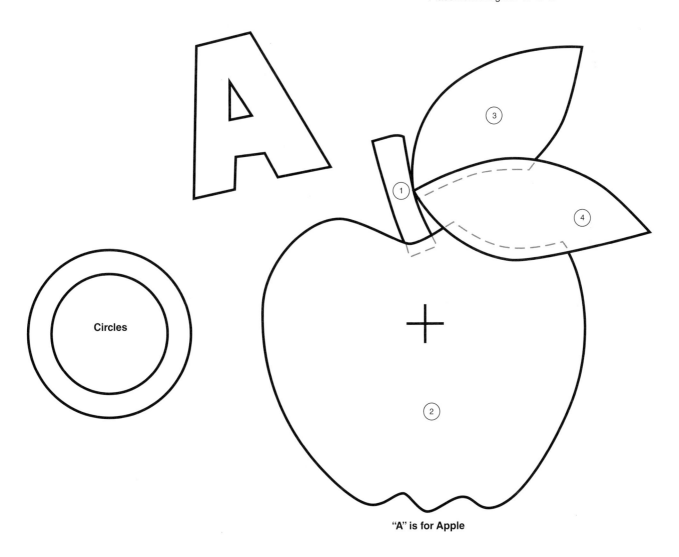

Circles

"A" is for Apple

Wool Appliqué

Project Note

For this wool appliqué project, all the design elements are applied to the background. There is no piecing—only applied wool and embroidery.

Finished Size

Quilt Size: 10" x 10"

Materials Needed

- Various wool scraps for circles and corner squares
- Scraps green wool for leaves
- Scrap brown wool for stem
- 1 (10" x 10") square background wool
- 1 (6" x 6") square red wool for apple and letter A
- 4 (2" x 6") rectangles green wool for borders
- 4 (2½" x 2½") squares orange wool for corner squares
- Wool backing 10" x 10"
- Pearl cotton or embroidery floss
- Embroidery needles
- Fray Check (optional)

Pattern:

"A" is for Apple

Instructions

1. Prepare templates from patterns on page 47.

2. Center the apple on the background and pin in place. Tuck the stem under the apple.

3. Using an embroidery needle and heavy pearl cotton or embroidery floss, stitch the apple and stem to the background using whatever stitch or stitches you desire, referring to Figure 2. *Note: The sample was stitched with a blanket stitch using black pearl cotton.*

Figure 2

4. Finish the apple design by adding and stitching the leaves and the letter A.

5. Place the background wool piece over the backing wool. Pin layers together.

6. Layer the borders and corner squares and circles onto the background fabric and stitch in place, referring to the placement diagram.

7. Hand-quilt, using the pearl cotton or embroidery floss, with large running stitches approximately ¼" away from the outer edges of the A and apple elements and inner edge of center square.

8. Finish with a label.

"A" is for Apple for Wool Appliqué
Placement Diagram 10" x 10"

Timely Tip

Pre-treat the cutting line with a little Fray Check if the wool appears to fray too much.

Shadow Appliqué

Finished Size
Quilt Size: 10" x 10"

Materials Needed
- Scraps green fabrics for leaves and stem
- Scrap black fabric for letter A
- 1 (6½" x 6½") square background fabric
- 1 (4½" x 4½") square red fabric for apple
- 4 (2½" x 2½") squares background fabric for corner squares
- 4 (2½" x 6½") rectangles purple fabric for borders
- 1 (6½" x 6½") square organdy
- Batting 14" x 14"
- Backing 14" x 14"
- 2¼" x 42" strip binding fabric
- Embroidery floss and needle

Pattern:
"A" is for Apple

"A" is for Apple With Shadow Appliqué
Placement Diagram 10" x 10"

Instructions
1. Prepare your appliqué design and fabric, referring to Shadow Appliqué technique on page 14.

2. Note the placement numbers on the Apple design. These show you which design element must be placed first.

3. Complete the appliqué, referring to Shadow Appliqué technique on page 14.

4. Assemble the quilt as shown in Figure 1 on page 45, adding borders and corner squares.

5. Layer the top, batting and backing. Stitch close to shapes through the organdy to hold in place. Finish with binding and a label. ❖

Persian Flower

The 3-D Persian Flower design is an abstract design representing a whimsical flower that does not exist in nature—it is pure fantasy!

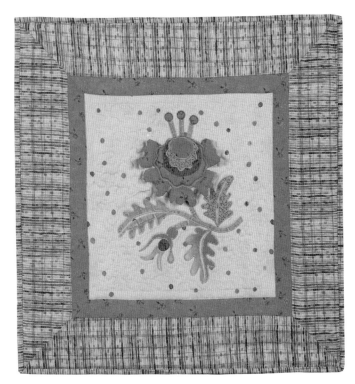

Materials Needed
- Assorted scraps of apple green and deep rose for flowers and leaves
- 12½" x 12½" pink background square
- ⅛ yard bright pink fabric for first border
- ⅝ yard pink multicolored stripe fabric for second border and binding
- Backing 28" x 28"
- Batting 28" x 28"
- Neutral-color all-purpose thread
- 6" x 6" square freezer paper
- ½ yard lightweight fusible webbing
- Small amount of fiberfill for stuffing petals
- Basic sewing tools and supplies

Pattern
Persian Flower

Cutting
1. Cut two 1½" by fabric width strips bright pink fabric.

2. Cut two 3½" by fabric width strips pink multicolored stripe fabric.

3. Cut three 2¼" by fabric width strips pink multicolored stripe for binding.

Persian Flower
12" x 12" Block
Make 1

Project Notes
The flower shape used in the Persian Flower design has petals that have been lightly stuffed with fiberfill to make them dimensional. The stuffed petals are inserted under the edges of the center flower shapes before the center is fused and then machine-stitched in place.

Project Specifications
Quilt Size: 20" x 20"
Block Size: 12" x 12" finished
Number of Blocks: 1

Appliqué Block

1. Trace each of the five petal shapes onto the freezer paper, adding ⅛"–¼" to the open bottom edge of the flower petal to insert under the flower center.

2. Layer the petal scraps with right sides together; press the traced freezer paper onto the wrong side of the layered fabric as shown in Figure 1.

Figure 1

3. Increase the number of stitches per inch on your sewing machine. Sew around each of the petal shapes on the traced lines through freezer paper and fabric layers, leaving the straight edge of each petal unstitched as shown in Figure 2. Remove freezer paper.

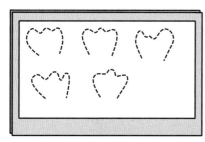

Figure 2

4. Cut around each of the petals leaving ⅛" beyond the stitching lines as shown in Figure 3; turn right side out through bottom opening.

Figure 3

5. Lightly stuff each petal with the fiberfill; baste the openings closed as shown in Figure 4.

Figure 4

6. Referring to Fusible Web Technique, trace all other pieces onto the paper side of the fusible webbing, leaving a space between pieces. Cut apart, leaving a margin around each one.

7. Fuse shapes to the wrong side of the appropriate color scrap fabric; cut shapes on traced lines. Remove paper backing.

8. Prepare a plastic overlay of the design, referring to page 8; pin the plastic overlay onto the background square. Slip the prepared pieces under the overlay for correct placement, slipping the stuffed petals under the flower center as shown in Figure 5; pin in place.

Figure 5

9. Check the placement of the overlapping parts; adjust, if necessary. When satisfied with placement, fuse pieces in place. Stitch in place using fused appliqué techniques on pages 13–19.

Adding Borders

1. Join one 1½" bright pink strip with one 3½" pink multicolored stripe strip with right sides together along length; press seam toward the wider strip. Cut the stitched strip in half to make two 21" strips. Repeat with second set of strips to make two more 21" strips.

2. Center a 21" strip on each side of the fused center square; stitch a strip to each side of the appliquéd center block, stopping stitching ¼" from the end of the block as shown in Figure 6 on page 50. Press seams toward strips.

50

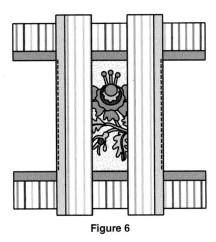

Figure 6

3. Fold back the stitched unit on the diagonal with right sides together as shown in Figure 7; draw a line from the end of the stitched line at a 45-degree angle to the outside edges, again referring to Figure 7.

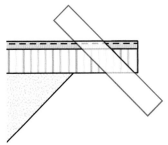

Figure 7

4. Stitch on the marked line; trim seam to ¼" beyond stitching and press open to complete the mitered corner.

5. Repeat steps 3 and 4 on each corner to complete the pieced top.

Finishing

1. Prepare the quilt top for quilting, referring to Finishing the Quilt on pages 20–23.

2. Using thread to match fabrics and a close satin stitch, machine-stitch around fused shapes through all layers to appliqué and quilt in one step.

3. Quilt and bind edges, again referring to Finishing the Quilt on pages 20–23. ❖

Timely Tip

A mitered corner makes a perfect corner finish when using a striped fabric in the borders.

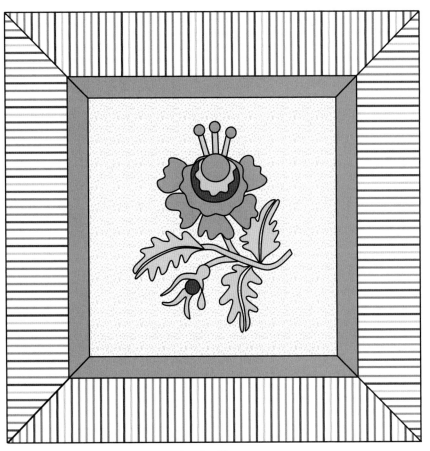

Persian Flower
Placement Diagram 20" x 20"

Persian Flower

House of White Birches, Berne, Indiana 46711 Clotilde.com

Cornucopia With Strawberries

This classic-style medallion quilt combines and illustrates most of the various techniques seen and used to create prizewinning, appliquéd quilts—clearly defined and interesting appliqué shapes, good contrast and interesting borders.

Materials Needed
- Assorted dark print scraps for pieced border squares at least 3" square
- 5" x 5" square blue print for Outer Flower and Berries
- 5" x 5" square dark print for one Inner Flower and Small Flower Centers
- 5" x 5" square rust print for Cornucopia details
- 9" x 9" square dark fabric for Cornucopia
- ⅛ yard off-white fabric for Small Flowers
- ¼ yard medium green fabric for block stems
- ½ yard light green fabric for leaves and border stems
- ½ yard medium red fabric
- ⅔ yard red pin-dot fabric for Strawberries, border and binding
- 1 yard light red fabric for background and borders
- Backing 45" x 45"
- Batting 45" x 45"
- All-purpose thread to match fabrics
- Basic sewing tools and supplies

Patterns:
Cornucopia
Outer Flower
Inner Flower
Large Flower Center
Small Flower
Small Flower Center
Strawberry
Berry
Leaf 1
Leaf 2
Leaf 3
Leaf 4
A Triangle

Project Notes
The luscious center of this quilt is an original appliqué block that is 15" square. With the addition of the corner triangles, the center medallion is 21" square finished. The first border is made of 3" pieced squares. The quilt is finished with an appliqué border that echoes the shapes, color and patterns of the center block. The result is a quilt design that is unified with interesting color harmonies and complementary rhythms. The appliqué in this sample is worked by hand and machine.

Project Specifications
Quilt Size: 37" x 37"
Block Size: 15" x 15" finished
Number of Blocks: 1

Cutting

1. Cut one 15½" x 15½" A square light red.

2. Cut two 11½" x 11½" squares medium background; cut each square in half on one diagonal as shown in Figure 1 to make four B triangles.

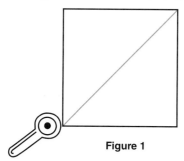

Figure 1

3. Cut (32) 2⅝" x 2⅝" C squares, assorted dark print scraps.

4. Prepare a template for the D/E triangle; cut 68 light red D and 60 medium red E triangles.

5. Cut four 4" x 27½" F strips, light red (second border).

6. Cut four 4" x 4" G squares light red.

7. Cut four 2" x 42" H/I strips red pin dot (third border).

8. Cut four 2¼" x 42" strips red pin dot (binding).

Freezer-Paper Instructions:

Center Block

1. Make 32" of ¼"-inch finished bias strips from the medium green fabric, referring to Stems & Vines on page 15.

2. Prepare one Outer Flower, one Inner Flower, one Large Flower Center, five Small Flowers and Small Flower Centers, five Strawberries, two Berries, two Leaf 1, two Leaf 2, 11 Leaf 3 and 13 Leaf 4 for appliqué using one of the techniques explained in Freezer-Paper Techniques, pages 9–11.

3. Lightly mark or press centering lines on the light red A square, referring to Figure 2. Use a light box to trace the design onto the background square using placement guides on pages 58–61.

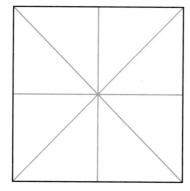

Figure 2

4. Reverse-appliqué the 5" x 5" square rust print to Cornucopia as shown in Figure 3 and referring to Reverse Appliqué, page 16. Trim away excess fabric when appliqué is complete and use to make flower centers.

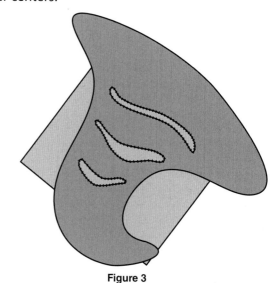

Figure 3

5. Arrange the appliqué pieces on the block in numerical order; baste in place, referring to Figure 4.

Figure 4

6. Stitch the appliqué pieces to the background using preferred stitch (see pages 16–19). When this step is complete, remove basting and all marking lines.

54

7. Sew a medium red B corner triangle to opposite sides of center. Sew triangles to remaining sides, referring to Figure 5. Press seams toward B. Trim the completed center to 21½" x 21½" square.

Figure 5

Pieced Border Units

Note: The border units will be 3½" x 3½" before they are sewn together for the border.

1. Sew a light D triangle to adjacent sides of a dark C square as shown in Figure 6. Repeat for all 32 squares. Press seams toward D.

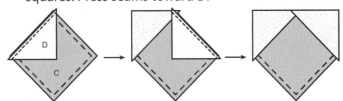

Figure 6

2. Sew medium E triangles to remaining sides of 28 C squares, as shown in Figure 7. Press seams toward E.

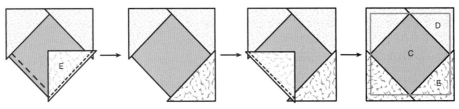

Figure 7

3. For corner units, sew a light D triangle to the three sides of the four remaining C squares; then sew a medium E triangle to remaining side as shown in Figure 8. Press seams toward D and E.

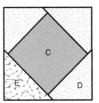

Figure 8

4. Sew seven units together as shown in Figure 9; repeat. Press seams open. Sew strips to opposite sides of center with the medium red fabric E triangles toward the center as shown in Figure 10.

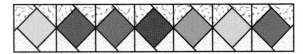

Figure 9

Figure 10

5. Sew nine units together with the corner units at each end as shown in Figure 11; repeat. Press seams open. Sew strips to top and bottom as shown in Figure 12; press again lightly.

Figure 11

Figure 12

Appliqué Border

1. Make 88" of light green ½"-wide finished bias strips for long stems. Cut into four strips each 22" long.

2. Prepare 24 Leaf 3, four Small Flowers and four Small Flower Centers for appliqué using the same method used in step 2 for Center Block.

Hint: To make two-color leaves, sew two 1"-wide green strips together; press seam open. Place template on strip so center tips of leaf lines up on seam line; cut out, leaving ¼" seam allowance.

3. Fold each F border strip in half along the length and width; press fold in place as shown in Figure 13.

Figure 13

4. Arrange a 22" bias stem along each of the long folds; baste in place. Continue arranging appliqué pieces on border strips, referring to Figure 14, and baste in place.

Figure 14

5. Stitch appliqué in place using your preferred stitch; lightly press.

6. Sew an appliqué border strip to opposite sides of quilt top.

7. Sew G corner squares onto the two remaining appliqué border strips, then sew to top and bottom of quilt.

Finishing

1. Measure and cut red pin-dot border strips, referring to Borders on pages 20–21. Sew a red border strip onto quilt sides first, then to top and bottom. Press border toward outside of quilt.

2. Refer to Finishing the Quilt on pages 20–23. Quilting on sample was added around the edges of all of the appliqué pieces, in the leaves and ¼" inside border squares. A leaf design, combining Leaves 1, 2 and 3, was marked and quilted in the large corner triangles of the center square, referring to Figure 15.

Figure 15

3. Bind edges, again referring to Finishing the Quilt on pages 20–23. ❖

Cornucopia with Strawberries Quilt
Placement Diagram 37" x 37"

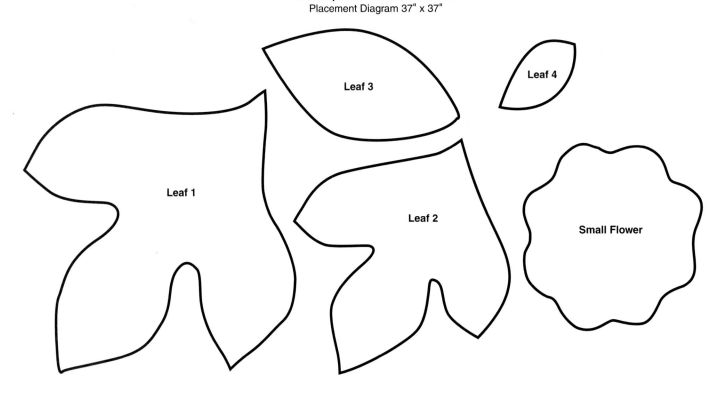

Leaf 4

Leaf 3

Leaf 1

Leaf 2

Small Flower

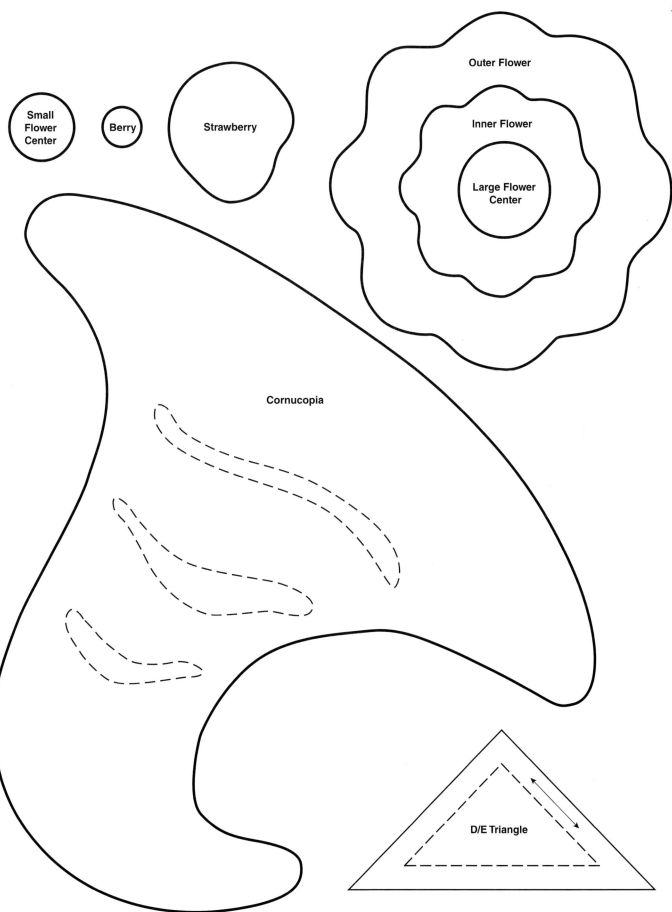

Small Flower Center

Berry

Strawberry

Outer Flower

Inner Flower

Large Flower Center

Cornucopia

D/E Triangle

House of White Birches, Berne, Indiana 46711   Clotilde.com

58

Pattern B

Center

Learn To Do Appliqué in Just One Weekend

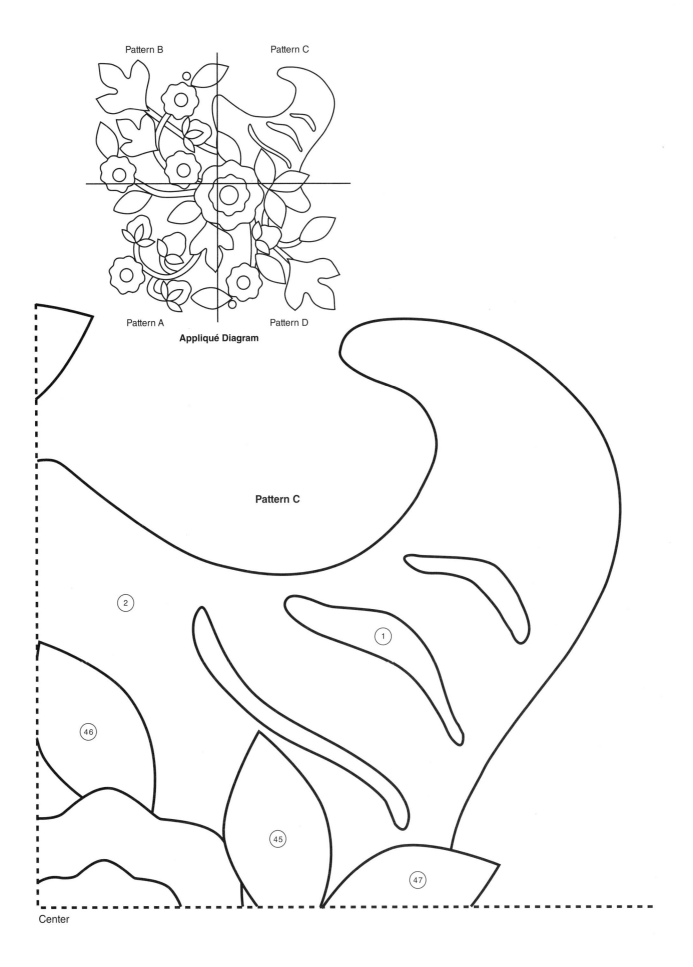

Pattern B

Pattern C

Pattern A

Pattern D

Appliqué Diagram

Pattern C

② 2

① 1

㊻ 46

㊺ 45

㊼ 47

Center

House of White Birches, Berne, Indiana 46711 Clotilde.com

Center

Pattern A

Center

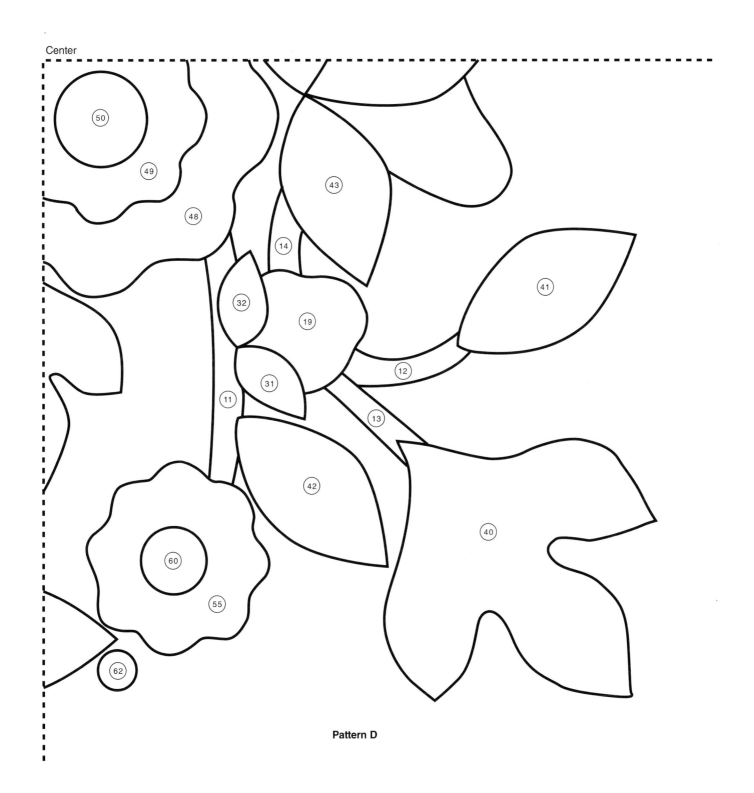

Pattern D

Tea Time

This whimsical teapot design illustrates what one can do with a well-defined shape and some interesting fabrics.

Project Notes

The teapot and the corner sashing squares are the same fabric. The center flower is cut and appliquéd from a large print fabric.

The appliqué was first fused then stitched down with a narrow black machine blanket stitch. The quilt was completed with machine quilting.

Project Specifications

Quilt Size: 14" x 16"

Materials Needed

- Scraps black checkerboard fabric, red print, white and fabric for flower
- 1 (7½" x 10½") light background fabric
- 1 (5½" x 10½") rectangle green background fabric
- 1 (8" x 10") rectangle yellow fabric for teapot and corner squares
- ¼ yard black fabric for sashing, binding and appliqué details
- Batting 22" x 24"
- Backing 22" x 24"
- ½ yard fusible webbing
- Basic sewing tools and supplies

Pattern

Tea Time

Making the Quilt Top

1. Sew the light and green background fabrics together along the 10½" measurement to form a 10½" x 12½" background rectangle, referring to Figure 1. Press seam open.

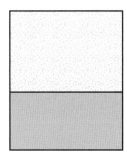

Figure 1

2. Referring to Fusible-Web Technique on page 12, prepare parts of the Teapot, Steam, and the Letters. **Note:** *The illustration is reversed for the fusing technique.*

3. Referring to the Placement Diagram, arrange the elements on the background rectangle. Notice that the teapot is slightly tilted. Fuse in place following the manufacturer's guidelines.

4. Appliqué the pieces in place using a narrow blanket stitch and black thread on top and in the bobbin, referring to Figure 2.

Figure 2

5. Cut two 2½" by fabric width strips from the black print for borders. From these strips cut two rectangles 2½" x 10½" and two rectangles 2½" x 12½".

6. Sew shorter rectangles to the top and bottom of the quilt as shown in Figure 3. Press seams toward the rectangles.

Figure 3

7. Cut four squares 2½" x 2½" from yellow fabric.

8. Sew squares to the ends of the remaining black border rectangles. Press seams toward black rectangles.

9. Sew remaining border pieces to the quilt. Press seams toward borders.

Finishing

1. Layer backing, batting and quilt top. Buttonhole-stitch around the center of the quilt and across the background rectangles.

2. Quilt as desired.

3. Cut two 2¼" by fabric width strips binding fabric; prepare binding, referring to Finishing the Quilt on pages 20–23.

Fast Finishing Triangles for Hanging

1. Cut two 3½" x 3½" squares from background fabric. Fold in half on the diagonal as shown in Figure 4.

Figure 4   **Figure 5**

2. Pin raw edges of the triangles to the upper back of the quilt along the corner seam lines as shown in Figure 5.

3. Bind quilt including the corner triangles in the binding seam.

4. Finish with a label. ❖

Tea Time
Placement Diagram 14" x 16"

House of White Birches, Berne, Indiana 46711   Clotilde.com

background seam

Tea Time